On the Future of Our Educational Institutions

Other Titles of Interest from St. Augustine's Press

On the Future
of Our Educational Institutions

Friedrich Nietzsche

Translated and Introduced by Michael W. Grenke

A William of Moerbeke Translation
Stuart D. Warner, General Editor

St. Augustine's Press
South Bend, Indiana
2004

1 2 3 4 5 6 7   11 10 09 08 07 06 05 04

Library of Congress Cataloging in Publication Data
Nietzsche, Friedrich Wilhelm, 1844–1900.
    [Über die Zukunft unserer Bildungsanstalten. English]
    On the future of our educational institutions / Friedrich
    Nietzsche; translated and introduced by Michael Grenke.
        p.   cm. – (William of Moerbeke translation series)
    Includes bibliographical references and index.
    ISBN 1-58731-601-3 (hard cover : alk. paper)
    1. Nietzsche, Friedrich Wilhelm, 1844–1900 – Views on educa-
    tion. 2. Educational change – Germany. I. Title. II. Series.
LB775.N547N53 2004
370'.1 – dc22   2004000797

∞ *The paper used in this publication meets the minimum requirements of the
American National Standard for Information Sciences – Permanence of Paper
for Printed Materials, ANSI Z39.48-1984.*

CONTENTS

TRANSLATOR'S NOTE

In translating *Über die Zukunft Unserer Bildungsanstalten*, it has been my intention to be literal and consistent. The motive behind my intention is a deep respect for the art and the thought of the author. I have tried to presume neither that I have understood Nietzsche completely nor that I can do better myself. One of the things most challenging and liberating about the writings of great philosophers is their ability to say unexpected things. I have tried to let those things be said.

I have striven to be consistent even with terms that I do not myself consider to be especially interesting or thematically important. Maybe someone else will find something worthwhile there. I have tried to produce a text that will not block the access of minds very different from my own. In as many ways as I could manage, I have tried to produce a text that looks like the German original and that says in English what Nietzsche says in German. If in instances, the text seems a bit awkward, or the reader is reminded that he is reading a translation, that is fine, so long as access to the sense of the matter is not blocked.

Still, it must be admitted that many choices had to be made along the way, and each one may have lost or obscured something of Nietzsche's meaning. I have not always been able to keep a one-word-for-one-word correspondence in translating, nor to translate words with equivocal meanings one way in all instances. I have not always kept Nietzsche's punctuation, though in instances where his punctuation is unusual, particularly in his use of dashes, I have been careful to keep it. I have not always kept his word order either. For one thing, the English-speaking mind does not easily wait until the end of the sentence for the verb. At times, I have translated words or phrases less literally for the sake of reading ease. Too often I have had to choose among a number of possible meanings for a word that might fit the context. I have documented many of these choices in my footnotes. Readers, in quoting from and thinking about the text, should feel free to adopt my more literal or alternative suggestions from the footnotes and consider that no offense to this translation.

The same applies to my most difficult and vexatious choice. A term of great prevalence in this text and of obvious thematic importance is a particularly difficult term to translate: Bildung. Bildung is a difficult term to translate under the best of circumstances, as it is a term that has a history of different technical uses, and the choice among them involves the translator in something of an act of interpretation. Bildung is typically rendered into English as "education," but also as "culture." Nietzsche complicates the matter by frequently employing the term Erziehung, sometimes in close proximity. Erziehung also means "education." That Nietzsche thought there to be some difference between the terms seems evident in the phrase "Erziehung zur Bildung" which I have translated as "education toward culture." It might have seemed best to translate Erziehung consistently as education and Bildung as culture, but not only did that seem wrong in a number of places ("cultural institutions," for instance, would be misleading), but Nietzsche's fairly frequent use of the Latin-based word Kultur seems to require translation as "culture." Erziehung means most literally a "drawing out, " and it is related to midwifing; in typical usage it applies to earlier education, and could be translated as "rearing." Bildung means most literally "formation," and it is connected to having an image [Bild] or form. Sorting out the different meaning of these terms is one of the major tasks that faces the reader of these lectures. I have not wished to impose an answer on the reader, but I have adopted the practice of translating Bildung as education in some places and as culture in others. The reader should feel free to substitute the other term in any case where they think it to be better. Wherever I have translated any other term as either "education" or "culture," I have included that term in brackets in the text. I have also included German terms in brackets at points to make the reader able to track connections that might otherwise not be apparent, such as plays on words. In certain cases bracketed German is included where I thought it might be helpful to those who have a smattering of German or a sensitivity for language.

There was also an apparent difficulty in translating the names of the German schools. There are not proper equivalents in English-speaking educational systems, so I have mostly left the terms untranslated. Although there are many regional differences, and there were more in Nietzsche's time, the German educational system about which Nietzsche is writing operates in something like the following manner. School begins with the Volksschule (literally the "people's school") at age six and lasts four years (five or six in some places). I have tended to translate Volksschule as "elementary school" as it is the most similar to English-speaking schools. A secondary level of schooling generally starts at age 11 when the students are divided into more and less academic paths. The two most important divisions for this text are between the Gymnasium and the Realschule. Those headed for the university go to the Gymnasium, which tends to give them a rigorous and broad liberal-arts education. I have not translated Gymnasium, but I have made the term plural in English fashion by adding an 's.' Those heading to a technical or specialized school [Fachschule] go to the Realschule (literally the "real school"). It did not seem readable to add an 's' to Realschule, so I have kept the German plural Realschulen where it occurs.

To establish the text, I have primarily relied upon the critical editions of Giorgio Colli and Mazzino Montinari, the *Kritische Studienausgabe* and the *Kritische Gesamtausgabe* (de Gruyter: Berlin, 1967–). Their text is based upon Nietzsche's handwritten manuscript. Other editions were consulted at some points. The *Gesammelte Werke* (Musarion Verlag: Munich, 1922) was used primarily for Appendix C.

Translator's Introduction

This text, *On the Future of Our Educational Institutions*, is a philosophic dialogue, more than one hundred pages long, written by Friedrich Nietzsche. It has a picturesque and myth-surrounded setting, up in the mountains along the Rhine. It has a rich set of characters: an old, grey philosopher; a middle-aged school teacher; two pistol-toting, young eavesdroppers; an awaited old friend; and a dog. It has action: shooting, shouting, singing, wrestling, a star falling, a torch-lit procession, a musical signal, and, of course, biting. And it has a most serious subject, education or culture.

It was to be Nietzsche's second book. Following hard upon the publication of *The Birth of Tragedy*, Nietzsche offered a series of six public lectures in the auditorium of the Museum at the University of Basel under the auspices of the "Freiwillige Akademische Gesellschaft."[1] The first five lectures were delivered on January 16th, February 6th and 27th, and March 5th and 23rd of 1872. Reports have the lectures attended by a large and distinguished crowd that included Jacob Burckhardt and, for the second lecture, Richard and Cosima Wagner. One day before delivering the fifth lecture, Nietzsche sent a letter to his then publisher, Ernst Fritzsch, offering the lecture series as his second book. Fritzsch accepted the offer,[2] but then a couple of weeks later, Nietzsche

1   The "Voluntary Academic Society."
2   See Fritzsch's letter to Nietzsche on April 4, 1872 in Appendix A. William Schaberg reads Fritzsch's response as a polite refusal (*The Nietzsche Canon*, The University of Chicago Press, 1995, p.32). This does not seem consistent with Fritzsch's assurance that "even the assigned completion date of manufacture I can hold to with a speedy

announced that their business together could not go forward, as he had now decided to rework the lectures and cast them in a different form. As Nietzsche expressed it later in a letter, "I can make everything better in a couple of years and want to make it better."[3] Nietzsche never went on to deliver the sixth promised lecture, nor, so far as is known, did he ever write it.[4]

In his letters, Nietzsche gives some accounts of his dissatisfaction with the lectures. He wrote to Malwida von Meysenbug in November of 1872 "it does not go enough into the depths and is dressed up in a farce whose invention is quite inferior." And then in December he wrote her: "One acquires a dry throat from these lectures and in the end nothing to drink!" But failure to go into the depths and leaving the reader with a dry mouth may not have been wholly unintentional. Everything seems to be building up toward the arrival of the old philosopher's friend. The lack of the sixth lecture may be responsible for the lack of something to drink. In February of the next year he wrote Malwida: "those lectures are primitive and in addition somewhat improvised." This may be because the writing of the lectures was rushed. With the first lecture in mid-January, Nietzsche spent the Christmas vacation alone to work on them. On December 3, he wrote his mother and sister that he was still "hardly able to think about" the lectures. Even in mid-February, after two of the lectures had already been delivered,

delivery of the manuscript," or with his request for advice from Nietzsche on how to circumnavigate the difficulty that would attend the fact that Fritzsch's press did not usually publish books on such subject matter. Moreover, Nietzsche's response to Fritzsch (letter in the second half of April) does not seem to understand Fritzsch's answer to have been a refusal. Nietzsche writes of "our business" having to be delayed as Nietzsche has decided to rework the material. See Thomas Heilke, *Nietzsche's Tragic Regime*, Northern Illinois Press, 1998, p. 139.

3   Letter to Malwida von Meysenbug, February, 1873.

4   From his notes, it evident that Nietzsche at times thought of writing a seventh lecture as well. Whether the seventh lecture was planned all along but not announced is unclear.

Nietzsche wrote Rohde that he was still "organizing and regenerating" the lectures. But it is not so unusual, in Nietzsche's career at least, to produce very fine works very rapidly.

However justified Nietzsche's critical self-assessment of the deficiencies of his lectures may be, it may not tell the whole story about his decision not to publish *On the Future of Our Educational Institutions*. In some measure, Nietzsche was clearly happy about the lectures. He privately distributed them to some of his closest and most respected acquaintances, including those to whom he expressed his highly self-critical views. Nietzsche did not complain when others made copies of his lectures and distributed them. He expressed delight when he heard the lectures were being read in Florentine society, where much pedagogical reform was under way. He knew of a plan to translate the lectures and publish them in Italian newspapers and did not seem to oppose that plan. Some sharing of these lectures with others, Nietzsche did not oppose.

The most important story here may not be the deficiencies of these lectures, but the way in which Nietzsche thought about publication and the standards he had in mind. For Nietzsche, publication is a question of conscience. "I have sworn to allow no book to appear with respect to which I do not possess a conscience as pure as a Seraphim. But it does not stand thus with respect to these lectures: they should and could be better."[5] But the question of conscience may not simply be the question of the intrinsic quality of the writing and thinking. Nietzsche may have worried at least as much about the quality of the readers as he worried about the quality of his writing. "Speaking strictly what I had devised for the last lecture – a very wild and colorful scene illuminating the night – was not fit for my Basel public, and it was certainly wholly well that for me the speech remains stuck in my mouth."[6] In a note, Nietzsche writes of "his original precaution," "which was previously directed at generally holding the public at a distance from this book, and thought to make its effect dependent alone upon a private distribution to good and worthy readers" (8[84]).

5   Letter to Malwida von Meysenbug, February, 1873.
6   Letter to Malwida von Meysenbug, December 1872.

Moreover, it seems that Nietzsche did not in fact abandon this project. In a way, this text, *On the Future of Our Educational Institutions*, did become Nietzsche's second book. Nietzsche wrote Erwin Rohde in April of 1872 that his lectures were to be published only "after a complete reworking." In August of 1872, Nietzsche wrote Carl Gersdorff that he was in fact reworking the lectures, and on the same day, Nietzsche solicited advice from Rohde regarding the reworking. There is some reason to think that the next book Nietzsche published, *Untimely Meditations*, is the reworking of *On the Future of Our Educational Institutions*. Some of the material is hardly reworked at all. Two passages, in two separate *Meditations*, each about a paragraph in length, are borrowed, nearly verbatim from these lectures.[7] But *On the Future of Our Educational Institutions* is not just the preliminary draft of the *Untimely Meditations*. *On the Future of Our Educational Institutions* may mark a decisive epoch in Nietzsche's development. Curt Paul Janz writes "With these lectures Nietzsche decisively turned upon the path, upon which we will see him up until the end."[8]

But even beyond this, *On the Future of Our Educational Institutions* is a dizzying interpretive puzzle. Here we find Nietzsche experimenting with a form that will match his principles regarding publicity. The form of narrative dialogue may have been chosen as an attempted solution to the problem of distributing texts to suitable readers. "Dialogue is the perfect conversation, because everything one of the parties says acquires its particular color, its sound, its accompanying gestures *strictly with reference to the other* to whom he is speaking, and thus resembles what occurs in correspondence, where one and the same man shows ten kinds of expression of his soul, accordingly as he writes now to this one, then to that one."[9] Of this dialogue, Nietzsche writes, "It is hortatory

---

7   See *David Strauss, the Confessor and the Writer*, section 4 and *Schopenhauer as Educator*, section 6.

8   *Friedrich Nietzsche Biographie*, Deutscher Taschenbuch Verlag, 1981, Volume 1, p.444.

9   *Human, All Too Human*, vol. 1, section 374.

throughout and in comparison with the 'Birth' popular or exoteric."[10] Both Nietzsche's Introduction and his Preface ask that the reader exercise a certain art of careful reading. The reader must "read the secret between the lines" and "guess what could only be suggested, complete, what must be concealed." In an echo of the Socratic doctrine that learning is recollection, Nietzsche writes for readers who "only need to be reminded, not to be instructed."

Writing for those who already, in a way, know may seem strange, but the matter may not be as simple as that. An openly or transparently exoteric text does not merely exclude the uninitiated, it entices them to seek initiation. The opening conceit of Nietzsche's lectures, his framing story, is that he has no wisdom of his own to offer, but he once heard something wise and can now repeat it as an ear-witness. This framing story provides for the author a distance from the text; he is not responsible for its claims or contentions. But the contrivance that the conversation was overheard by eavesdroppers lends an atmosphere of pregnant attentiveness that is likely to spread to the listeners and readers. The mood of eavesdropping is that of careful, attentive striving to hear. Nietzsche not only hides from the readers but also draws them in. He not only writes for special readers but also encourages readers to become special.

In a way this work is an education [Erziehung] toward culture [Bildung], in that it is a drawing out [Erziehung] that aims at formation [Bildung] through the use of images [Bilden]. These images consist in a lively setting and a complex set of characters, along with a fair number of symbolic allusions. And these images contribute greatly to the atmosphere of secrecy and hidden things. Here are "joys and jokes not understandable for every man." Here we are told "precisely that which lies before all eyes as a monstrous riddle is understood by the fewest as a riddle." But exactly the openness with which these hidden things are identified as secrets calls to us eavesdroppers to creep closer and to listen more attentively.

10   Letter to Erwin Rohde, March 15, 1872.

The setting is appropriate to this complex scheme. The mountainous region is out away from prying eyes, yet it affords exceptional views. The place where the two twosomes have their encounter is such that it first makes the important speech, the old philosopher's, into a droning natural music and later into something intrusive and articulate. First it is a mysterious sound in the background, then an intelligible sound very much in the foreground. The forest conceals much, and yet it has special openings through with the characters can see exactly what they need to see. The coming of night makes the two parties descend, but it also reverses the natural order of who should lead whom, and it makes the torch-lit procession and the shooting star visible.

The mystery and magic of both myth and music abound. Rolandseck is associated with the hero Roland. The Drachenfels is the location of Siegfried's battle with a dragon.[11] The mention of Loyal Eckart reminds of the hero sagas. Nietzsche is under the influence of Wagner. Music permeates the atmosphere, some seemingly made by nature, some by instruments, some by voice, and some by pistol. There is a conductor at the beginning and the image of a conductor at the end. In this magical atmosphere both anything is possible; and everything is infused with symbolic meaning.

The characters serve to add to the puzzle. With whom should the reader identify? Whom can the reader trust? Who speaks for Nietzsche? An old grey philosopher is the main speaker. Can he be Nietzsche's spokesman? Even with a "young Nietzsche" standing by? Is this old man a proper model? He is capable of making mistakes. He can be a bit forgetful or oblivious. He is devoted to philosophic wonder, but he also indicates that horror is a proper starting point for philosophy. Perhaps nausea and anger[12] are also included in his example as possible starting points. He has a dog that seems

11 A note sketching the sixth lecture (18 [5]) has "Battle in the cave." This is seemingly a reference to the cave wherein Siegfried slew the dragon. Drachenfels means "dragon rock."

12 It is worth noting that the narrating Nietzsche calls the old philosopher's anger a defect in Lecture IV.

to have something of a philosophic character; it barks with presentiment, but it also makes mistakes and it bites. Maybe a philosophy that can begin with horror is necessarily potentially dangerous. But is it possible for a philosophy that attends to the future of "our"[13] educational institutions not to begin with horror? Furthermore, must not all real philosophy attend to education, to culture?

Does that mean that all real philosophy must make some kind of alliance with violence? Certainly pistols play a large role in this narrative. Pistol-shooting is the cover story that young Nietzsche and his friend employ to get away from their fellow students; thus pistol-shooting is linked to their cultural aspirations, perhaps not merely to provide those aspirations with a smoke screen. The old philosopher opposes the boys' pistol-shooting twice, first when he mistakenly thinks they are dueling, second when they are merely being noisy. The noise produced by the pistol-shooters is characterized as "a true assassination attempt against philosophy." Yet later, the art of pistol shooting is enlisted to respond to the musical signal. The philosopher asks the boys to fire and only complains when they fail to keep the beat. The old man tells the boys, "one must know what one wants when one handles weapons." The boys are not to shoot at the falling star, because it "collapses already by itself." But what are they to shoot at? The young Nietzsche carves a pentagram into the stump for a target, and nature assists his efforts by making the target grow bigger. Is this enlarging of the target nature's approval? Were the boys, unawares, doing the right thing all along? The world that opposes the great Schiller in Goethe's *Epilogue to Schiller's 'The Bell''* is the "stumpfen" world. The "stupid" world is the "stumpy" world.

13 Nietzsche's explicit interest in this dialogue is the German educational system, but the applicability of his thoughts on education is much wider. Even here, Nietzsche does not focus on German education out of love of Germany, but only as a means to classical education. Nietzsche seems to think one must start where one is and get an organic and living sense for "the classical" before one can properly approach classical antiquity – "With a leap into the blue no one comes into antiquity" (Lecture II).

For the old philosopher, education, culture, is a matter of the highest priority. Culture comes first, before the state, before religion, and surely before the stupid world. Now what happens when one puts education first? Then to the extent to which the state, for instance, affects education, the state must be changed to accommodate the needs of education. Perhaps many people think they make education the highest priority, but this old philosopher shows where that principle ultimately leads. If the needs of education are great enough and the state is interfering (and what state does not interfere?), then the state must be overthrown. One must "prepare for battle with the barbarism of the present" and perhaps "transform the Gymnasiums into the arsenals and workshops of this battle." This may explain the references to and qualified praise of such revolutionary texts as Schiller's *Robbers* and such revolutionary secret societies as the Burschenschaft. Those who think educational reform can be enacted in a substantial way without a restructuring of the state either happen to live in very culture-friendly state or do not put education first. But even a state friendly to culture is not enough. The state must be subordinate to culture; it must be culture's servant. What happens if one puts culture first? Perhaps one then has to learn to conduct not only orchestras but also young men with guns.

It is perhaps sad that we were never given a concluding lecture. The friend awaited by the old philosopher, by everyone – characters, listeners, and readers alike – only approaches but never appears. We do not get to hear the real conversation, the dialogue that would not be a waste of time for the philosopher. We do not get to listen in while all the secrets are revealed. On the other hand, perhaps we are not really missing here that which we truly need. When he thinks his friend is not going to show up, the old philosopher exclaims, "We were here so long for nothing" (Lecture IV). This provokes the two young eavesdroppers to leap from hiding and entreat the old philosopher to go on. Clearly the young students are deeply moved by what has been said. And the philosopher's companion, too, despite his greater years joins in the entreaty. Perhaps for those of us who are more like the young students than like the old philosopher, this dialogue ends just as it should: with great thirst and no drink, only an image of what we might need before we were ready to drink.

On the Future of
Our Educational Institutions
Six Public Lectures[1]

---

1   Only the first five of the lectures were ever written and delivered. A
     seventh lecture seems at one point to have been planned.

INTRODUCTION

The title that I have given my lectures should have been, as is the duty of any title, as precise, clear, and penetrating as possible; but it has, as I now mark quite well, from an excess of precision turned out too short and therefore it has again become unclear, so that I must begin thereby to explain this title and thereby the task of these lectures before my honored listeners and, indeed, if need be apologize. When I promised thus to speak on the future of our educational institutions, I was not at all thinking primarily about the special future and further development of our Basel institutions of this kind. As frequently as it may indeed appear that my general statements allow themselves to be exemplified exactly in our indigenous educational institutions, I am not the one that makes these exemplifications and hence would like to bear just so little of the responsibility for practical application of such a kind: precisely on the ground that I hold myself much too foreign and inexperienced, and I feel myself much too little firmly rooted in the local conditions in order to judge rightly such a special configuration of educational circumstances [Bildungsverhältniße][2] or even in order to be able to sketch with some certainty their future. On the other hand,[3] I am all the more conscious of the place in which I have to deliver these lectures, in a city namely, which seeks to advance culture [Bildung] and education [Erziehung] in a disproportionately [unverhältnißmäßig] grandiose sense and with a standard that is downright shaming for larger states: so that I certainly do not make

2   Verhältniße means more literally "relations" or "proportions," as in unverhältnißmäßig, translated below as "disproportionately."

3   More literally, "On the other side."

a mistake when I suppose that here where one *does* so much more for these things one also *thinks* about them so much more. But exactly that must be my wish, indeed my presupposition, to stand here in spiritual intercourse [geistiger Verkehr] with listeners who have reflected on education [Erziehung] and questions of education [Erziehungsfragen] just as much as they are willing to advance in deed what they have recognized as right: and only before such listeners will I, with the greatness of the task and the shortness of the time, be able to make myself understood – if they, namely, instantly guess what could only be suggested, complete, what must be concealed, if they generally only need to be reminded, not to be instructed.

While I must thus decline throughout to be considered as an unbidden giver of advice in Basel school- and education-questions [Erziehungsfragen], I think still less of prophesying from out of the whole horizon of the civilized peoples [Kulturvölker] of today on a coming future of education and of educational means: in this monstrous vastness of the circle of vision my view is blinded, as it likewise becomes uncertain in an all-too-great nearness. Under *our* educational institutions I understand accordingly neither the special Basel, nor the countless forms of the farthest of all peoples spanning the present, rather I mean the *German institutions* of this kind, in which we have indeed rejoiced here. The future of these German institutions should concern us, i.e., the future or the German Volkschule, of the German Realschule, of the German Gymnasium, of the German university: whereby we meanwhile refrain from all comparisons and evaluations and especially protect ourselves from the flattering delusion as if our conditions, with regard to other civilized peoples, were exactly the universal model and unsurpassed. Enough, they are our educational schools, and they do not accidentally hang together with us; they do not hang around us like a garment: rather as living monuments of significant cultural movements, in some formations even "the household effects of our ancestral fathers,"[4] they tie us to the past of the people

4   This phrase is borrowed from Goethe, *Faust*, I.408.

and are in the essential characteristics such a holy and honorable legacy that I know how to speak of the future of our educational institutions only in the sense of the highest possible approximations to the ideal spirit out of which they were born. Thereby it stands firm for me that the countless transformations that the present time has permitted in these educational institutions in order to make them "timely" ["zeitgemäß"][5] are for a good part only distorted courses and deviations from the originally elevated tendency of their foundation: and what we in this respect dare to hope from the future is such a universal renewal, refreshing, and purification of the German spirit that out of it even these institutions will be in a certain measure new born and then after this new birth appear at the same time old and new: whereas they now most of all claim only to be "modern" and "timely."

Only in the sense of that hope do I speak of a future of our educational institutions: and this is the second point about which I must, with an apology, be up front and explain myself. It is the greatest of all presumptions to want to be a prophet, so that it already sounds laughable to explain that one does not want to be it. It is permitted to no one to examine [vernehmen] in the tone of prophecy the future of our education and thereby a connected future of our educational [Erziehungs] means and methods, if he can not prove that this future education, in whatever measure, is already in the present and has only to spread around him [um sich greifen] in a much higher measure in order to be able to exercise a necessary influence upon schools and educational [Erziehungs] institutes. One suffers me only, like a Roman haruspex,[6] to divine the future out of the viscera of the present: which, in this case, wants to say not more and not less than to promise the victory one day to an educational tendency already at hand even if it is presently

---

5 The title of Nietzsche's second published book was *Unzeitgemäßige Betrachtungen, Untimely Meditations.*

6 A haruspex was a kind of diviner or augurer of Etruscan origin, early introduced into the Roman religion who, among other methods, told the future from examination of the entrails of sacrificial victims.

at the moment not liked, not honored, not widespread. It will be victorious, however, as I assume with the highest confidence, because it has the greatest and most powerful ally, *nature*: whereby we surely are not permitted to conceal that many of the presuppositions of our modern educational methods carry in themselves the character of the unnatural and that the most disastrous weakness of our present is connected precisely with these unnatural educational methods. Whoever feels through and through at one with this present and takes it as something "self-evident" ["Selbstverständliches"], that one we envy neither regarding this faith nor regarding the scandalously refined [gebildet] fashionable term "self-evident": but whoever arrives at the opposite standpoint, already in despair, indeed that one no longer needs to fight and may simply surrender oneself to solitude in order to be alone soon. Between these "self-evidencers" and the solitaries stand however the *fighting ones*, that is the ones rich with hope, as their noblest and elevated expression our great Schiller stands before our eyes, just as Goethe portrays him for us in his *Epilogue to the Bell*:[7]

> Now glowed his cheek red and redder
> From that youth, that never flies away from us,
> From that courage, that, sooner or later,
> Conquers the opposition of the stupid world,
> From that faith, that ever increases
> Now boldly issues, now patiently yields,
> So that the goodness may work, grow, profit,
> So that the day of the noble finally may come.[7]

That which has been said by me up till now may be accepted by my honored listeners in the sense of a foreword, the task of which should only be to illustrate the title of my lectures and to protect it against possible misunderstandings and unjustified demands. In order now immediately, at the entrance of my considerations [Betrachtungen], going over from the title to the matter, to circumscribe the general circle of thought from out of which a

---

7 Nietzsche quotes here lines 49–56 of Goethe's *Epilogue to Schiller's "The Bell."*

judgment on our educational institutions should be attempted, a clearly formulated thesis, at this entrance, should like a blazon, remind everyone dropping by of whose house and farmstead he is treading into in concept: provided he does not, after consideration of such a blazon, prefer to turn back from such a thereby marked house and farmstead. My thesis runs:

Two apparently opposed streams, in their working equally ruinous and in their results finally flowing together, rule in the present our educational institutions, which were originally grounded upon wholly other foundations: first the drive after the highest possible *extension of education*, on the other side the drive after *the diminution and the weakening of the same*. According to the first drive education should be carried into an ever wider circle; in the mind [Sinne] of the other tendency it will be expected of education that it give up its highest claim to self-mastery and subordinate itself serving another form of life, namely that of the state. In respect to these disastrous tendencies of extension and of diminution it would lead hopelessly to despair if it were not possible at any time whatsoever to help to victory two opposing tendencies, truly German and generally having a rich future, that is the drive after the *narrowing* and *concentration* of education, as the opposite of a greatest possible extension, and the drive after the *strengthening and self-sufficiency* of education, as the opposite of its diminution. But that we have faith in the possibility of a victory, thereto we are justified by the knowledge that both those tendencies of extension and diminution run against the eternally same intention of nature just as equally as a concentration of education upon the few is a necessary law of the self-same nature, is generally a truth, whereas those two other drives may only succeed to found a false culture [Kultur].

PREFACE,[8]

to be read before the lectures,
although it does not genuinely apply to them.

The reader, from whom I expect something, must have three qualities: he must be at rest and read without haste, he must not always be bringing himself and his "education" in between, finally he should not expect at the conclusion, as a result for instance, tables. Tables and new curricula for Gymnasiums and Realschulen I do not promise, I marvel much more at the superpowerful nature of those who are in a position to traverse the whole course, from out of the depths of empiricism up to the heights of the genuine problems of culture, and again down there in the lowlands of the driest regulations and of the most elegant tables; but I am satisfied, if I, in the midst of gasping, have climbed a passable mountain and permitted myself to delight in the free view, even if in this book I should never be able to satisfy the friends of tables.

I daresay I see a time coming, in which serious human beings, in the service of a wholly renewed and purified culture [Bildung] and in common labor, indeed, again become the legislators of everyday education [Erziehung] – of education [Erziehung] toward that new culture [Bildung]; probably they will then again make tables – but how distant is the time! And what must have occurred

8   This preface was placed before the text of the lectures by the editors of the *Kritische Studienausgabe*. It was found in a folder with other material belonging to *On the Future of Our Educational Institutions*. Nietzsche later reworked this preface somewhat and included it in *Five Prefaces to Five Unwritten Books*, under the title *Thoughts on the Future of Our Educational Institutions*.

in between! Perhaps lying between it and the present is the annihilation of the Gymnasium, perhaps even the annihilation of the university or at least such a total reformation of the so-called educational institutions that their old tables might present themselves to later eyes like remainders out of the time of the lake-dwellings.[9]

The book is designed [bestimmt] for calm readers, for human beings who are still not swept up in the dizzying haste of our rolling age and who still do not feel an idolatrous pleasure in being crushed by its wheels – that is, for few human beings! These, however, cannot get accustomed to estimate the value of everything according to whether it is time-sparing or time-wasting, these "still have time"; to them it is still allowed, without feeling reproach before themselves, to select the good hours of the day and their fruitful and powerful moments and to seek together to reflect on the future of our education, these may even believe they have spent their day in a right useful and worthy manner, namely in the *meditatio generis futuri*.[10] Such a human being has still not unlearned how to think while he reads; he still understands how to read the secret between the lines; indeed he is of such a wasteful type that he even still reflects over that which was read perhaps long after the book itself has left the hands. And indeed not in order to write a review or another book, but only in order to reflect! A wastrel worthy of punishment! He who is calm and unconcerned enough to be able to set out together on a distant way with the author, whose goal will first be shown in full clarity to a much later generation! If against that the reader, violently excited, immediately springs furiously to the deed, if he wants to pluck the fruit from the moment, which whole generations may hardly take by force, then we must fear that he has not understood the author.

Finally, the third and most important demand is that he in no case, after the manner of the modern human being, be permitted to bring himself and his education in between without pause as, so to speak, a secure measure and criterion of all things. We wish

9   Nietzsche refers to the early human settlements consisting of houses on stilts built in or along lakes.

10   Latin for "contemplation of the genus of the future."

much more that he may be educated enough in order rightly to think little of his education, indeed to despise it; then he may with the greatest trust leave himself to the leading of the author, to whom it is permitted to dare, exactly from not-knowing and from knowledge about not-knowing, to speak thus to him. Nothing other does he want to claim for himself than a strongly inflamed feeling for the specific character of our present German barbarism, for that which so noteworthily distinguishes us as barbarians of the nineteenth century from barbarians of other times.

Now he seeks, with this book in hand, after such who will be driven hither and yon by a similar feeling. Let yourselves be found, you isolated ones in whose existence I believe! You selfless ones, who suffer in yourselves the suffering and destruction of the German spirit, you contemplative ones whose eyes do not perhaps grope about with hasty peering at the exterior of things, but know how to find the approach to the kernel of their essence, you high-minded ones, of whom Aristotle says in praise that you go through life hesitating and deedless, except where a great honor and a great work clamor after you![11] You I call up! Only this time do not crawl away into the holes of your seclusion and your mistrust! At least be a reader of this book in order afterward to make it, through your action, be annihilated and forgotten! Think you it is determined to be your herald: when you yourself, in your own armor, appear upon the battlefield, who might still crave then to look back at the herald who called you?

---

11   Here Nietzsche uses Hochsinnigen to refer to Aristotle's μεγαλόψυ-
      χος, the great-souled man. See *Nicomachean Ethics*, 1124b 24–26.

LECTURE I

My honored listeners,
The theme about which you have in mind to reflect with me is so
serious and important and in a certain sense so disquieting, that
even I, like you, would go to anyone that promised to teach anything about the same, should that one be ever so young, even
should it seem in itself quite improbable that he would himself
accomplish, out of his own powers, something sufficient and suitable to such a task. It would still be possible that he had *heard*
something right about the disquieting question of the future of our
educational institutions that he now again wanted to recount to
you; it would be possible that he had distinguished teachers
[Lehrmeister] to whom it may be more fitting to prophesy on the
future and indeed, similarly to the Roman haruspices, out of the
viscera of the present. Indeed you have something of this kind to
expect. I was at one time, through odd but fundamentally quite
harmless circumstances, an ear-witness to a conversation which
noteworthy men conducted on just that theme and have imprinted
the main parts of their meditations, and the whole manner and way
which they treated this question, much too firmly in my memory
not to fall always into the self-same rut whenever I reflect about
similar things: only that I occasionally do not have the confident
courage that those men before my ears and to my astonishment
proved to have at that time not only in the bold expression of for-
bidden truths but also in the still bolder construction of their own
hopes. All the more it appeared useful to me to fix finally for once
such a conversation in writing in order also to incite others still to
judgment about such conspicuous views and remarks: – and hereto

I believed myself on special grounds to be permitted to use precisely the occasion of these public lectures.

I am of course quite conscious in what sort of place I recommend a general reflection and consideration, in a city namely which seeks to advance in a disproportionately grandiose sense the culture [Bildung] and education [Erziehung] of its citizens, up to a standard that must have about it something downright shameful for greater states: so that I also certainly do not make a mistake here with this supposition that here, where one *does* so much more for these things, one also *thinks* about them so much more. Precisely only to such listeners, however, will I, with the retelling of that conversation, be able to be fully understandable – such who immediately guess, what could only be suggested, complete, what must be concealed, who generally need only to be reminded, not instructed.

Now hear, my listeners, my harmless experience and the less harmless conversation of those not yet named men.

We transpose ourselves right into the situation of a young student, that is into a situation that, in the restless and violent movement of the present, is something downright unbelievable, and that one must have experienced in order generally to consider possible such an unconcerned self-lulling, such a trifling, almost timeless, comfort in the moment. In this situation I passed, together with a similarly aged friend, a year in the university city of Bonn on the Rhine: a year which, through the absence of all plans and purposes, detached from all future designs, carries in itself something almost dreamlike for my present perception [Empfindung] whereas the same on both sides, before and after, is framed by periods of growth. We both remained undisturbed although we lived together with an association [Verbindung] that was numerous and fundamentally excited by and striving after other things; occasionally we had trouble satisfying or declining the somewhat too lively demands of these our contemporaries in age. But even this play with a contrarily striving element now has, when I put it to myself before my soul, still a similar character to many checks that everyone experiences in the dream, for instance when one believes oneself able to fly, but feels oneself drawn back by inexplicable hindrances.

I had, along with my friend, numerous memories from the earlier period of growth, from our common time in the Gymnasium, and *one* of the same I must point out more specifically, because it forms [bildet] the transition to my harmless experience. On an earlier trip on the Rhine, which had been undertaken in late summer, I had, together with that friend, thought out a plan almost at the same time and at the same place – and indeed each for themselves – so that we felt compelled by this unusual coincidence to carry it through. We resolved at that time to found [stiften] a small union of a few comrades, with the intention to find for our productive inclinations in art and literature a firm and obligatory organization: i.e., expressed more plainly: it must make it binding on each of us to submit from month to month a product of our own, whether it be a poem or an essay or an architectural project or a musical production, concerning which product now each of the others was entitled to make, with unlimited openness, a friendly critique.[12] Thus through reciprocal supervision we thought just as much to excite our educational drives as to keep a tight rein on them:[13] and really the result was even of the kind that we must always retain a thankful, indeed a ceremonious, feeling [Empfindung] for that moment and that place which had given us that inspiration.

For this feeling [Empfindung] the right form was soon found, in which we reciprocally obligated ourselves, whenever it may be possible to seek out, on that day, in any year, the lonely spot by Rolandseck,[14] in which we at that time, sitting next to one another in thought, immediately felt ourselves inspired to the same resolution. Taken strictly, this obligation was indeed not rigorously enough observed; but precisely on this account, because we had

---

12 It is known that in his time at the Gymnasium, Schulpforta, Nietzsche did form such a society, called "Germania," with, at least, Wilhelm Pinder and Gustav Krug.

13 More literally, "to keep hold on the reins."

14 Rolandseck (also known as Rolandswerth) is a small town on the Rhine. A story of newer origin held that Roland, Charlemagne's Paladin, had died here.

many sins of omission on the conscience, in that student year at Bonn, as we finally dwelt on the Rhine for some lasting time again, it was decided by us both with great firmness to satisfy this time not only our law, but also our feeling [Gefühl], our thankful excitement and to visit [heimzusuchen][15] on the right day the place by Rolandseck in a solemn way.

It was not made lightly by us: for precisely on this day the numerous and lively student association, which hindered us from flying,[16] was quite busy and pulled with all its powers on all the threads that could hold us down. Our association had resolved on a great festive excursion to Rolandseck at this point in time, in order to secure one more time its collected members at the close of the summer half-year and to send them home afterward with the best memories of their parting.

It was one of those perfect days, like those, in our climate at least, only just this late summer time is able to beget: heaven and earth thronging calmly in unison next to one another, wonderfully mixed together out of summer warmth, autumnal freshness, and blue infinity. In the most colorful, fantastical attire, in which, with the gloominess of all other fashions, the student alone may still amuse himself, we boarded a steamship that was festively covered in streamers in honor of us and planted our association's flag on its deck. From both banks of the Rhine a signal shot sounded from time to time, according to our direction, through which the inhabitants of the Rhine as well as, before all, our host in Rolandseck would be informed of our approach. I tell nothing now of the noisy procession from out of the landing place through the excited-curious region. Equally as little of the joys and jokes not understandable for every man that we tolerated among one another; I pass over a feast that was gradually moving, indeed becoming wild, and an unbelievable musical production in which, now through individual performances, now through collective performances, the whole group at the table must have participated, and which I, as musical

15 More literally, "to seek home."
16 Perhaps an allusion to the dream flying three paragraphs earlier.

adviser of our association, had earlier to rehearse and now to direct. During the finale, somewhat wild and becoming ever faster, I had already given my friend a wink and immediately after the final chord, similar to howling, we both disappeared through the doors: behind us to a certain extent a howling abyss slammed shut.

Suddenly quickening, breathless, natural silence. The shadows already lay somewhat broader, the sun glowed unmovingly, but already sunk low, and from the greenly glittering waves of the Rhine a gentle breeze wafted over our hot faces. Our consecrated memory only originally obligated us for the later hours of the day, and there-fore we had thought to fill the last bright moments of the day with one of our solitary hobbies in which we were so rich at that time.

We were accustomed at that time to shoot pistols with a pas-sion, and in a later military career this technique was of great use to each of us. The servant of our association knew our somewhat dis-tant and elevated shooting place and had carried our pistols there for us in advance. This place was located on the upper edge of the wood that covered the lower range of hills behind Rolandseck, upon a little uneven plateau and indeed completely in the vicinity of the place of our foundation and consecration. On the wooded slope, sideways from our shooting place, there was a little, tree-free place, inviting one to sit down, which granted a view away over the trees and shrubs toward the Rhine, so that precisely the beautiful winding lines of the Seven Mountains[17] and before all the Drachenfels[18] delimited the horizon against the groups of trees, whereas the glittering Rhine itself, holding the island Nonnenwörth[19] in its arms, formed [bildete] the middlepoint of

17   The Siebengebirge are seven young volcanic mountains along the Rhine. Many legends are associated with the Seven Mountains, each of which, according to legend, is the body of a giant.

18   Literally, Drachenfels means "dragon rock." It is one of the Seven Mountains, a truncated cone of trachyte with castle ruins upon it. It is supposedly the place where Siegfried slew the dragon in its cave [Drachenhöhle].

19   Nonnenwörth is an island on the Rhine near Rolandswerth. At one

this rounded aperture. This was our place, consecrated by common dreams and plans, to which we wanted to, nay must, withdraw in a later evening hour, supposing we wanted to conclude the day in accord [im Sinne] with our law.

Sideways of that, upon that little uneven plateau, stood not far a powerful stump of an oak, solitary on the otherwise tree- and bush-less plane and setting off the low undulatory elevations. On this stump we had once, with united strength, carved a distinct pentagram that, in the weather and storm of the last years, was still more burst open and presented a welcome target for our pistol art. It was already one of the later afternoon hours, as we arrived at our shooting place, and from out of our oak stump a broad and pointed shadow leaned in over the meager heath.[20] It was very still: we were hindered by the high trees at our feet from seeing toward the Rhine into the depths. Soon the sharp echoing noise of our pistol shots rang, all the more shocking in this solitude – and I had just dispatched the second bullet toward the pentagram as I felt myself seized violently on the arm and at the same time saw also my friend, in the process of loading, interrupted in a similar way.

As I quickly turned myself around, I looked into the angered face of an old man, while I felt at the same time as if a powerful dog had furiously sprung on my back. Before we, – namely me and my comrade, likewise disturbed by a second, somewhat younger man – collected ourselves for any words of wonderment whatsoever, the speech of the gray old man already resounded in threatening and violent tones.

"No! No!" he called to us, "Here there will not be dueling! It is least permitted to you, you studying youths! Away with the pistols! Let it rest, be reconciled, shake hands! How can this be? These would be the salt of the earth, the intelligence of the future, the seed of our hopes – and these cannot for once make themselves free from the crazy catechism of honor and its principle of the

time it had a Benedictine cloister, but since 1850 it has housed a school for young girls.

20   Here Nietzsche uses an archaic spelling "Haide" for "Heide."

justice of the fist? I do not want to tread thereby too near to your heart, but it does your heads little honor. You, whose youth retains the speech and wisdom of Hellas and Latium[21] as nurse, and upon whose youthful spirit one has born inestimable care to allow the light-rays of the wise and noble of beautiful antiquity to fall at an early time – you want to begin with this, so that you make the codex of knightly honor, i.e., the codex of folly [Unverstands] and of brutality, the guiding principle of your conduct? – Indeed look at it rightly for once, bring it into clear concepts, discover its pitiful limitedness and let the touchstone for it be not your heart but your understanding. If you do not reject this now, then your head is not qualified to work in the field where the necessary requirements are an energetic power of judgment, which shreds the bonds of prejudice easily, and a rightly impressive understanding, to be able to separate purely the true and the false even there where the difference lies deeply concealed and is not, like here, to be grasped with the hands: so in this case, my good ones, seek after another honorable way to come through the world, become soldiers or learn a handicraft that has a golden soil."

At this blunt, although true, speech we answered excitedly, in that we constantly reciprocally cut each other short: "First, you err in the main point; for we are here in no case in order for us to duel but in order for us to practice in shooting pistols. Second, you appear not at all to know how it goes with a duel: Do you think that we would set ourselves against one another, like two highwaymen, in this solitude, without seconds, without physicians etc.? Third, finally we have regarding the question of dueling our own viewpoint[22] – each for himself – and do not want to be assaulted and frightened by correction of your kind."

This certainly not-polite reply had made an evil impression upon the old man; while at first, as he marked that no duel was in question, he looked friendlier upon us, our concluding turn vexed him so that he grumbled; and as we even ventured to speak of our

21 Greece and Rome, respectively.
22 More literally, "standpoint."

own viewpoints, he seized his companion violently, quickly turned himself around and shouted bitterly to us "One must have not only viewpoints but also thoughts!" And, the companion interjected: "Show respect, even if such a man sometimes errs!"

However in the mean time my friend had already loaded again and shot anew at the pentagram while he shouted: "Look out!" This instantaneous rattle behind his back made the old man furious; once again he turned himself around, looked at my friend with hatred and said then with a tender voice to his younger companion: "What should we do? These young men are ruining me through their explosions."

"You should of course know," began the younger one who had turned toward us, "that your exploding pleasures are in the present case a true assassination attempt against philosophy. Observe this honorable man – he is in a position to ask you not to shoot here. And if such a man asks –"

"Why, one quite probably does it," the gray old man interrupted him and looked at us sternly. –

At bottom we did not rightly know what we had to think of such proceedings; we were not clearly conscious of what our somewhat-noisy pleasures had in common with philosophy; we realized just as little wherefore we, out of incomprehensible considerations of politeness, should give up our shooting place and may have stood there in this moment quite undecided and annoyed. The companion saw our momentary bewilderment and explained to us the details. "We are compelled," he said, "to wait a couple of hours here in your immediate proximity, we have an appointment according to which a distinguished friend of this distinguished man wants to meet here even this evening; and indeed we have chosen for this gathering a quiet place with a few benches here in the wood. It would not be pleasant if we are continually startled here by your neighboring shooting practice; it is for your own sensibility [Empfindung], as we presuppose, impossible to shoot here any further when you hear that it is one of our first philosophers who has sought out this quiet and remote solitude for a reunion with his friend." –

This explanation [Auseinandersetzung][23] disturbed us all the more: we saw now a still-greater danger than only the loss of our shooting place approaching us and asked hastily: "Where is this quiet place? Surely not here to the left in the wood?"

– Precisely this is it. –

"But this place belongs this evening to the both of us," my friend interjected. "We must have this place," we both shouted.

Our celebration, resolved upon long ago, was momentarily more important to us than all the philosophers of the world, and we expressed our feeling [Empfindung] so animatedly and excitedly that, with our desires, unintelligible in themselves but so pressingly expressed, perhaps we looked somewhat laughable. At least our philosophical intruders looked at us laughingly and questioningly, as if we now should speak to excuse ourselves. But we were silent, for we wanted least of all to betray ourselves.

And thus both groups stood dumb opposite each other, while over the tops of the trees lay the red of evening continuing to pour out. The philosopher looked at the sun, the companion at the philosopher, and we both at our hiding-place in the wood that should be endangered thus for us precisely today. A somewhat grim feeling came over us. What is any philosophy, we thought, when it hinders being by oneself and enjoying oneself alone with a friend, when it holds us down from becoming philosophers ourselves. For we believed our celebration of our memory to be of precisely an authentic philosophical nature: with it we wished to set serious designs and plans for our further existence; in solitary reflection we hoped to find something which should in the future form [bilden] and satisfy our innermost soul in a similar way to that former productive activity of the earlier years of our youth. Precisely in that should that authentic act of consecration consist; nothing was resolved but precisely this – to be alone, to sit there reflectively, thus like that time five years before as we collected ourselves in

23 Auseinandersetzung is notoriously difficult to translate; here it might also mean something like "confrontation." Literally, it means "setting apart from one another."

common to that resolution. It should be a silent celebration, all memory, all future – the present naught but a dash in-between. And now a hostile fate stepped into our magic circle – and we did not know how it was to be removed: indeed we felt, with the peculiarity of the whole encounter, something mysteriously exciting.

While we stood by one another for a long time, dumb thus, separated into hostile groups, the evening clouds above us reddened all the more and the evening became ever quieter and milder, while we almost overheard the regular breathing of nature, as it concluded its day's work, satisfied with its work of art, the perfect day – a tumultuous confused cry of jubilation ripped through the middle of the twilight [dämmerende] silence ringing up from the direction of the Rhine; many voices became loud in the distance – that must have been our fellow students who probably now wanted to travel around in boats on the Rhine. At that we thought that we would be missed and had missed something ourselves: almost at the same time with my friend I raised the pistol: the echo threw our shots back and together with it came also quite a well-known shouting, as a signal of recognition, from out of the depths. For we were equally as well known as we were infamous with our association as passionate pistol shooters.

In the same moment, however, we felt our behavior as the highest impoliteness against the dumb philosophical newcomers, who had up till now stood there in quiet meditation and had sprung to the side frightened at our double shot. We quickly stepped up to them and cried alternating: "Forgive us. Now was the last time for shooting and that holds for our comrades on the Rhine. They have understood it. Do you hear? – If you insist on having that quiet place here to the left in the bushes then you must at least allow that we also seat ourselves there. There are several benches there: we will not disturb you: we will sit quietly and will be silent: but seven o'clock is already at hand, and we *must* now go there."

"That sounds more secretive than it is," I added after a pause; "there is among us a serious promise to spend these next hours there; there are also grounds for that. The place is held sacred by us due to a good memory; it is also supposed to inaugurate a good future for us. We will therefore trouble ourselves to leave behind with you no bad memory – after we have indeed repeatedly disturbed and frightened you."

The philosopher was silent: however his younger companion said: "Our promises and appointments unfortunately bind us in the same way, not only for the same place but also for those same hours. We have now the choice whether we want to make some fate or a kobold[24] responsible for this encounter."

"Besides, my friend," the philosopher said, placated, "I am more satisfied with our pistol-shooting youths than before. Did you notice how quiet they were a little while ago as we looked at the sun? They did not speak, they did not smoke, they stood silently – I almost believe they reflected."

And with a quick turning to us: "*Did* you reflect? Tell me that while we go together to our common quiet place." We now took a few steps together and came, climbing downward, into the warm, damp atmosphere of the wood, in which it was even darker. In going there my friend unreservedly explained his thoughts to the philosopher: how he had feared that today for the first time he would be hindered from philosophizing by a philosopher.

The gray old man laughed. "How is this? You feared that a philosopher would hinder you from philosophizing? Such a thing may no doubt be found: and you have still not experienced it? Have you had no experiences at your university? And surely you hear philosophic lectures?" –

This question was uncomfortable for us; for such had not been the case at all. We even still had at that time the harmless belief that anyone who possessed the office and title of philosopher at a university was also a philosopher: we were quite without experiences and badly instructed. We said honestly that we still had heard no philosophical lectures [Kollegien], but would make up for the neglect yet.

– But what is it that you now call, he asked, your philosophizing?

24 A spirit in German folklore often haunting houses, sometimes helpful, but tricky.

"We are," I said, "at a loss for a definition. Indeed we probably mean approximately this much, that we want seriously to trouble ourselves to reflect on how we are best likely to become educated human beings."

"That is much and little," grumbled the philosopher: "Only reflect rightly thereon! Here are our benches: we want to place ourselves quite far asunder [uns recht weit auseinandersetzen]: I indeed do not want to disturb you from reflecting on how you are to become educated human beings. I wish you luck and – viewpoints, as in your duel question, viewpoints that are correct [rechte], your own, brand-new, and educated. The philosopher does not want to hinder you in philosophizing; only do not frighten him through your pistols. Imitate today for once the young Pythagoreans: these had to be silent for five years, as servants of a legitimate [rechten] philosophy – perhaps bring it up to date for five quarter hours even, in the service of your own future education, with which you are indeed so urgently occupied."

We were at our goal: our celebration of our memory began. Again as at that time five years before, the Rhine swam in a gentle mist, again, as at that time, the heavens sparkled, the wood smelt sweet. The most remote corner of a distant bench accommodated us; here we sat almost as if concealed and so that neither the philosopher nor his companion could look us in the face. We were alone; when the voice of the philosopher came over to us dampened, it had in the mean time, among the rustling movement of the foliage, among the buzzing noise of a thousandfold teeming existence in the heights of the wood, almost become a natural music; it acted as loud as a distant monotonous lament. We were really undisturbed.

And thus a time passed in which the evening red paled all the more, and the memory of our youthful educational undertaking rose up before us ever clearer. It appeared to us thus as if we should owe the highest thanks to that peculiar union: it had been to us not only a supplement for our Gymnasium studies but nothing short of the authentic fruit-bearing society within whose framework we had inscribed even our Gymnasium as a single means in the service of our general striving after education.

We were conscious that at that time we had never altogether thought about a so-called profession, thanks to our union. The ever-so-frequent exploitation of these years by the state, which as soon as possible enlists useful officials and wants to secure their unconditioned obedience through excessively exhausting examinations, had remained in the furthest distance throughout our educations: and how little anything of a utilitarian sense, anything with a view to quick advancement and a fast career [Laufbahn] had determined us, lay for each of us in the fact, appearing comforting today for once, that we both even now did not rightly know what we should become, indeed that we did not at all concern ourselves about this point. Our union had nourished in us this happy unconcernedness; precisely for it we were thankful right from the heart at our celebration of our memory. I have already said once that such a purposeless letting-oneself-delight in the moment [Moment], such a self-lulling, in the rocking chair of the blink of an eye [des Augenblick][25] must appear almost unbelievable, in any case blameworthy to our present, ill-disposed as it is toward every useless thing. How useless we were! And how proud we were to be so useless! We had been able to quarrel with one another about the fame of whom of the both of us was the more useless one. We wanted to make nothing clear, to ask for nothing, to aim at nothing, we wanted to be without a future, to be nothing other than stretched out good-for-nothings comfortable on the threshold of the present – and we even were it, Hail us!

– Thus of course it appeared to us at that time, my honored listeners! –

– Having indulged in these woeful self-meditations, I was approximately on the point of answering to myself now even the question of the future of *our* educational institution, as it gradually appeared to me that the natural music resounding from the distant bench of philosophers lost its former character and came over to us much more intrusively and more articulately. Suddenly I was

25 More literally "glance of an eye." Augenblick is the more usual German word for "moment."

conscious that I listened, that I eavesdropped, that I eavesdropped with a passion, listened with ears stretched forward. I nudged my perhaps-somewhat-tired friend and said to him softly, "Do not sleep! There is something there for us to learn. It attends to us, even if it is not intended for us."

I heard, namely, how the young companion defended himself rather excitedly, how against that the philosopher with an ever-more-forceful ring in the voice attacked him. "You are unchanged," he shouted at him, "unfortunately unchanged; it is unbelievable to me how you are still the same as seven years ago when I saw you for the last time, when I dismissed you with doubtful hopes. Your modern educational skin, which in the mean time has been hung over you, I must unfortunately again, not to my pleasure, remove – and what do I find under there? Indeed the same unchangeable 'intelligible' character, as Kant understands it,[26] but unfortunately also the unchanged intellectual [character] – which is probably also a necessity, but is a small comfort. I ask myself, why have I lived as a philosopher, when a whole year that you have spent in my company [Umgang], not with a stupid spirit and with a real lust to learn, has indeed left behind no clearer impressions! Now you conduct yourself as if you still had never, with regard to all education, heard the cardinal principle, to which I have so often come back in our earlier intercourse. Now what was the principle?" –

– "I remember," answered the scolded student; "You were accustomed to say there would be no human being striving after education if he knew how unbelievably small the number of really educated ones finally is and can be in general. And in spite of that even this small number of truly educated ones would not for once be possible, if a great mass, fundamentally against its nature and only directed by a tempting deception, did not involve itself with the education. One should therefore reveal nothing publicly of that laughable disproportion between the number of truly educated ones and the monstrously great educational apparatus; here is

26 A reference to Kant's division of the world into apparent things and "intelligible" things, things in themselves.

hidden the authentic secret of education: that, namely, countless human beings are struggling after education, working for education, apparently for themselves, but fundamentally only in order to make possible some few human beings."

"This is the principle," said the philosopher – "and indeed could you so forget its true sense, to believe yourself to be one of those few? You have thought that – I mark it well. But that belongs to the worthless signature of our educated present. One democratizes the rights of genius in order to be relieved from the personal task of education and need of education. It wants everyone to sit down where possible in the shadow of the tree the genius has planted. One would like to escape that difficult necessity to have to work for the genius in order to make his generation [Erzeugnung][27] possible. How is this? You are proud to want to be a teacher? You despise the jostling multitude of the learning ones? You speak with little esteem about the task of the teacher? And you would like then, within a hostile boundary of that multitude, to lead a solitary life, copying me and my way of life? You believe yourself to be able with a spring to reach immediately what I had to attain finally after long, stiff-necked struggle merely to be able generally to live as a philosopher? And you do not fear that the solitude will avenge itself on you? Merely attempt it, to be a hermit of education – one must have a surplus richness in order to be able to live off it for all things! – Extraordinary young ones! Precisely always the most difficult and most high, which has become only just possible for the master, they believe they must imitate: whereas precisely they should know how difficult and dangerous this is and how many excellent gifts could still perish therein."

– "I want to conceal nothing from you, my teacher," the companion said here. "I have heard too much from you and have been too long in your vicinity for me to be able to surrender myself, what is more, root and branch,[28] to our current cultural [Bildungs] – and

27 Erzeugen means "to produce" or "to reproduce." Erzeugniße is translated as "products" elsewhere.
28 More literally, "with skin and hair."

educational [Erziehungs] – system. I feel too clearly those unholy errors and abuses at which you were accustomed to point with your finger – and indeed I note a little of the power in me with which I would have, with a brave struggle, successes. A general lack of courage overcame me; the flight into solitude was not pride, not arrogance. I gladly want to describe to you, what signature I have found on the now so lively and intruding self-moving cultural [Bildungs] – and educational [Erziehungs] – questions. It appeared to me that I must distinguish two main directions, – two apparently opposed streams, in their working equally ruinous, in their results finally flowing together, rule the present of our educational institutions: at once the drive after the highest possible *extension* and *broadening* of education, then the drive after the *decrease* and *weakening* of education itself. On various grounds, education is supposed to be carried into the widest circles – the one tendency longs for that. Against that the other expects of education itself that it give up its highest, noblest, and most elevating claims and resign itself to the service of some one or other form of life, of the state, for instance.[29]

"I believe I have remarked from which party the call resounds most clearly for the highest possible extension and broadening out of education. This extension belongs among the beloved national economic dogmas of the present.[30] As much knowledge and education as possible – consequently as much production and demand as possible – consequently as much happiness as possible: thus or thereabouts runs the formula. Here we have utility as the goal and purpose of education, still more exactly acquisition, the highest possible winning of great amounts of money. From out of this direction education would roughly be defined as the insight, with which one keeps oneself 'up to date,'[31] with which one is familiar with all ways in which money can most easily be made, with which

29 Compare the last paragraph of the introduction.

30 The rest of this paragraph was, with slight changes, used by Nietzsche in *Schopenhauer as Educator*, section 6; KSA 1.387.23 – 388.25.

31 More literally, "upon the height of his time."

one masters all means through which the traffic between human beings and peoples goes. The authentic task of education according to that would be to form [bilden] to the highest degree possible 'courante' human beings, in the manner in that one calls a coin 'courant.'[32] The more there are such courante human beings so much happier a people is: and precisely that must be the intention of the modern educational institutes, to advance each so far as it lies in his nature to become 'courant,' to form each [aus zu bilden] such that he has from his measure of knowledge [Erkenntniss] and wisdom [Wissen] the greatest possible measure of happiness and success. Each one must be able to appraise [taxiren] himself exactly; he must know how much he has to exact from life. The 'alliance of intelligence and possession' which one maintains according to these views, almost counts as a moral [sittliche] demand. Any education is hateful here that makes solitary, that sticks goals above money and acquisition, that wastes much time: one is well accustomed to do away with such other educational tendencies as 'higher egoism' as 'immoral [unsittliche] educational Epicureanism.' To be sure, according to the morality [Sittlichkeit] prevailing here something of the reverse will be desired, namely a *speedy* education, in order to be able quickly to become a money-earning being and indeed such a thorough education in order to be able to become a *very much* money-earning being. Only so much culture [Kultur] will be permitted to a human being as is in the interest of acquisition, but so much will even be demanded of him. In short: humanity has a necessary claim to earthly happiness – for that reason education is necessary – but also only for that reason!"

"Here I want to insert something," said the philosopher. "With this not unclearly characterized view emerges the great, indeed monstrous, danger that the great masses at some time or other leap over the middle step and set off directly upon this earthly happiness. One now names that the 'social question.' Namely, it may appear thus to these masses, consequently, that for the greatest part of human beings education is only a means for the earthly happiness

32   French for "current," related to the English currency.

of the fewest: the 'most general education possible' weakens education so that it can confer no privileges whatsoever and no respect whatsoever anymore. The most general education is just barbarism. Nevertheless I do not want to interrupt your argument."

The companion went on: "There are still other motives besides that so beloved national economic dogma for the overall expansion and broadening of education, so bravely striven for. In some countries the anxiety in the face of a religious oppression is so general and the fear of the consequences of this oppression so marked that one meets with a thirsting lust for education in all the social classes and drinks in precisely the elements of the same that are wont to dissolve the religious instincts. Elsewhere, on the other hand, a state strives here and there, for the sake of its own existence, after the highest possible expansion of education because it always still knows itself strong enough to be able to clamp under its yoke even the strongest emancipation[33] belonging to education, and it has been found reliable whenever the most expanded education comes to good for its officials or its armies, finally always only for it itself – for the state – in rivalry with other states. In this case the foundation of a state must be just so broad and firm in order to be able still to balance the complicated vaults of education, as in the first case the tracks of an earlier religious oppression must still be felt enough in order to be pressed to such a dubious counter-measure. – Thus where only the war-cry of the mass longs after the widest education of the people, I am well accustomed to distinguish whether a luxurious tendency toward acquisition and possession, whether the brand of an earlier religious oppression, or whether the clever self-regard [Selbstgefühl] of a state has stimulated this war-cry.

"On the other hand, it would appear to me as if another tune [Weise] was struck up on various sides, indeed not so loudly but at least as emphatically, the tune of the *diminution of education*. One accustoms oneself to having something of this tune whispered in one's ear in all learned circles: the general fact that, with the

33 More literally, "being freed of chains."

exploitation of the scholar in the service of his science that is now striven for, the *education* of the scholar becomes ever-more accidental and more improbable. For the study of science is now so expanded in breadth that whoever, with good, although not extreme talents, still wants to achieve something in them, will pursue a completely specialized field, and then remain untroubled, however, by everything left over. If he should even now in his field stand above the *vulgus*,[34] in everything left over he indeed belongs to them, i.e., in all main things. Thus one learned in an exclusive field is then similar to a factory worker, who, his life long, makes nothing other than a specific screw or handle to a specific tool or to a machine, in which he then, to be sure, attains an unbelievable virtuosity. In Germany, where one understands to hang a glorious mantle of thought over even such painful facts, one probably quite admires this narrow moderation of field [Fachmäßigkeit] of our scholars and their ever-further deviation from the right education as a moral [sittliches] phenomenon: the 'trust in the small,' the 'carter-trust' become themes of splendor, being uneducated beyond one's field is paraded as a sign of noble modesty.

"There have passed centuries in which it was understood as self-evident [es sich von selbst verstand] that under the heading of an educated one [Gebildeten], one conceived of scholars and only scholars: from the experiences of our time one would with difficulty feel bound to such a naïve identification [Gleichstellung]. For now the exploitation of the human being for the sake of the sciences is without objection the overall accepted presupposition: who still asks himself what a science may be worth which so vampire-like consumes its creatures? The partition of work in science strives practically toward the same goal after which, here and there, the religions strive with consciousness: after a decrease of education, indeed after an annihilation of the same. However, what is a thoroughly justified desire for some religions, according to their genesis and history, must for science at one time or other lead up to a self-immolation. Now we are already at the point that in all general

34   Latin for "the common people."

questions of a serious nature, before all in the highest philosophical problems, the scientific human being as such indeed no longer can get a hearing: whereas that sticky binding stratum which has laid itself between the sciences, journalism, thinks to fulfill its task here and carries it out now according to its essence, i.e., like the name says,[35] as a day-laborer.

"In journalism, namely, both directions flow together: extension and diminution of education shake hands here; the journal treads precisely in the place of education, and whoever, even as a scholar, still now makes educational claims accustoms himself to rely upon that sticky stratum of mediation which cements the seams between all forms of life, all situations, all arts, all sciences, and which is so firm and reliable as even the daily paper is accustomed to be. In the journal culminates the educational aim of the present: just as the journalist, the servant of the moment, treads in the place of the great genius, of the leader for all times, or the redeemer of the moment. Now tell me yourself, my excellent master, what should I make my hopes in the struggle against an invasion of all authentic educational strivings that has reached everywhere, with what courage, as an individual teacher, may I proceed when I indeed know how the crushing roller of this pseudo-education would pass lightly over any freshly strewn seed of true education? Think how useless now the most exhausting work of the teacher must be, who perhaps would like to lead a student back into the endlessly distant and difficult-to-grasp world of the Hellenic, as into the authentic home of education: when indeed the same student will in the next hour grab after a newspaper or after a novel of the time or after one of those educated [gebildeten] books whose theory of style is already born in the nauseating arms of the present-day educational barbarism." –

– "Now hold silent for once!" the philosopher interjected with a strong and compassionate voice, "I conceive you better now and should have said no such evil word to you earlier. You are right in everything, only not in your lack of courage. I want to say to you now something to your consolation."

35   In old French, *journal* means "daily."

LECTURE II

My honored listeners! Those among you whom I am permitted to greet first, from this moment on, as my listeners and who have become aware, perhaps only as a rumor, of my lecture held three weeks ago, must now let it fall, without further preparation, to be led into the middle of a serious dialogue that I had begun to retell at that time, and today I will first remind about its last turns. The younger companion of the philosopher had just had to excuse in an honest-confidential way, before his distinguished teacher, why he had retired annoyed from his former teaching position and spent his days in a self-chosen solitude unconsoled. Least of all had a prideful conceit been the cause of such a resolve.

"Too much," said the righteous younger one, "have I heard from you, my teacher, too long have I been in your vicinity, in order for me to be able to give in faithfully to our prevailing cultural [Bildungs] and educational [Erziehungs] system. I feel too clearly those unholy errors and abuses at which you were accustomed to point with your finger: and indeed I note a little of the power in me with which I would have, with a brave struggle, successes, with which I could demolish the bulwarks of this alleged education. A general lack of courage overcame me: the flight into solitude was not pride, not arrogance." Thereupon he had, in his excuse, so described the general signature of this educational system that the philosopher could not help falling into speaking [in's Wort zu fallen][1] to him with a compassionate voice and thus to calm him. "Now hold silent for once, my poor friend," he said; "I conceive you better

1   More literally, "to fall into a word."

} 41 {

now and should have said no such hard word to you earlier. You are right in everything, only not in your lack of courage. I want to say to you now something to your consolation.[2] How long, probably, do you believe that that conduct of education in the schools of the present, which weighs so heavily upon you, will still last? I do not want to withhold from you my belief about that: its time is over, its days are numbered. The first, who will dare it, to be completely honest in this area will get to hear the reverberance of his honesty out of a thousand courageous souls. For fundamentally there is an implicit understanding among the more nobly endowed and warmer-feeling human beings of this present: each of them knows what he had to suffer from the educational conditions of the schools, each would like at least to save his descendents from the pressure, even if he himself had to be exposed. But the fact that despite that it nowhere comes to full honesty has its sad cause in the pedagogical poverty of spirit of our time; precisely here it lacks really inventive gifts, here the truly practical human beings are lacking, that is, those who have good and new notions and who know that the right genius and the right practice must meet necessarily in the same individual: whereas with the empty[3] practical human beings precisely notions and therefore again the right practice are lacking. Make yourself only once acquainted with the pedagogical literature of this present; in *him* there is nothing more to corrupt, who with this study is not horrified concerning the highest of all poverty of the spirit and concerning a truly clumsy circle dance. Here our philosophy must begin not with wonder [Erstaunen] but with horror [Erschrecken][4]: whomever it is not able to bring to horror is asked to leave his hands from pedagogical things. The reverse was of course the rule hitherto: those who were horrified shyly ran from there like you, my poor friend, and the

2   The summary ends here.

3   Nüchternen can mean also "sober," "sensible," "reasonable," "moderate," or "temperate."

4   Erschrecken is a strong word and could also be translated as or "terror." "Shock" is another, milder possibility.

empty ones who were not horrified laid their coarse hands right coarsely upon the most delicate technical science [Technik] of all that there can be in an art, upon the technical science of education. However, that will not be possible much longer; there may come at sometime an honest man, who has those good and new notions and for their realization dares to break with everything present-at-hand [Vorhanden], he may at sometime put before it, by a grandiose example, what those coarse hands, hitherto alone active, are not able to initiate – then they will at least generally begin to distinguish, then they will at least scent the opposition and be able to reflect on the causes of this opposition, whereas now so many still believe, in all good nature, that the coarse hands belong to the pedagogical handicraft."

– "I would like, my honored teacher," said here the companion, "for you to help me, by one single example, to that hope which speaks so courageously out of you to me. We both are familiar with the Gymnasium; do you believe, e.g., even with respect to this institution that here, with honesty and good, new notions, the old, stubborn habits could be dissolved? Here, namely, it appears to me, not to be a hard wall protecting against the battering rams of an attack, but probably the most fatal tenaciousness and slipperiness of all principles. The attacker does not have a visible and solid opponent to crush: rather this opponent is masked, is able to transform himself into a hundred forms and in one of the same to slip away from the clutching grasp, in order ever again to confound the attacker anew through cowardly giving way and tenacious rebounding. Precisely the Gymnasium has pressed me to a discouraged flight into solitude, precisely because I feel that if the struggle leads to victory here all other institutions of education must give way and that whoever must despair here must generally despair in the most serious pedagogical things. Thus, my master, instruct me about the Gymnasium: what hope may we have for an annihilation of the Gymnasium, what for a new birth of the same?" –

– "I also," said the philosopher, "think as highly as you of the significance of the Gymnasium: in the educational goal that is striven after by the Gymnasium all other institutes must measure themselves, in the strayings of *its* tendency they suffer too. Through the purification and renewal of the same, they themselves will likewise be purified and renewed. Such a significance as a motive center [Mittelpunkt] even the university can now no longer take up and claim for itself, which, with its present formation, at least according to *one* important side may be counted merely as an extension of the tendency of the Gymnasium; how, I want to make this clear to you later.[5] For now let us consider [betrachten] that which generates in me the hopeful opposition, that *either* the hitherto cultivated [gepflegte], thus motleyed and difficult-to-catch spirit of the Gymnasium will fully vanish in the air or that it must be purified and renewed from the ground up: and so that I do not shock you with general principles, let us think first of one of those Gymnasium experiences that we have all had and from which we all suffer. What is now, considered with a rigorous eye, *the German lesson*[6] in the Gymnasium?

"I will tell you first what it should be. By nature every human being speaks and writes now so badly and commonly their German language as is only possible in an age of newspaper German: therefore the growing-up, noble, gifted youth must be put with force under the glass bell of good taste and rigorous linguistic discipline: if this is not possible, from now on I prefer next to speak again Latin, because I am ashamed of such a bungled and disgraced language.

"What kind of task would a higher educational institution have at this point if not precisely this: authoritatively and with the appropriate rigor to lead the youths grown linguistically wild to the right way and to call out to them, 'Take your language seriously! Whomever it does not bring here to the feeling of a holy duty, in that one is present not even so much as a germ for a higher education. Here you can show how highly or how little you esteem art and how far you are related to art, here in the treatment of our mother tongue. If you do not attain so much from yourselves, to feel a physical nausea before certain words and turns of phrase of

5   This promise is taken up in the fifth lecture, p. 104.
6   Or "*German instruction.*"

} 44 {

our journalistic addiction, then merely give up striving after education: for here, in the nearest of all nearnesses, in every moment of your speaking and writing you have a touchstone[7] as to how difficult, how monstrous, the task of the educated one now is and how improbable it must be that many of you should come to the right education. –

"In the sense of such an address the German teacher at Gymnasium would have the obligation to make his students attentive to thousands of details and precisely, with the complete security of a good taste, to forbid the use of such words as e.g., 'to tax,' 'to pocket,' 'to make allowance for a thing,' 'to seize the initiative,' 'self-evident' – and so on *cum taedio in infinitum*.[8] The same teacher would further have to show in our classical authors from line to line how carefully and rigorously every turn is to be taken, when one has the right artistic feeling in the heart and the complete understanding of everything of which one writes before the eyes. He will ever and ever again compel his students to express the same thoughts still once more and still better and will find no limit to his activity before the ones little gifted are not got into a holy terror [Schreck] before the language, the gifted ones into a noble inspiration for the same.

"Now, here is a task for the so-called formal education and one of the most valuable of all: and what do we find now in the Gymnasium in the place of the so-called formal education? – Whoever understands how to bring under the right rubrics what he has found here will know what he has to think of the present Gymnasium as an alleged educational institution: namely, he will find that the Gymnasium, according to its original formation, educates [erzieht] not for culture [Bildung] but only for scholarship [Gelehrsamkeit] and further, that it lately takes the turn as if it does not even wish any longer to educate [erziehn] for scholarship but for journalism. This is to be shown in the manner that the German lesson is given, as in a right reliable example.

7 More literally, "proving stone."
8 Latin for "with tedium into infinity."

"In the place of that pure practical instruction, through which the teacher should accustom his student to a rigorous linguistic self-education [Selbsterziehung], we find over all the traces of a scholarly-historical [gelehrt-historischen] handling of the mother tongue: i.e., they proceed with it as if it were a dead language and as if there were no obligation to the present and future of this language. The historical manner has become for our time common up to the degree that even the living body of the language is surrendered to its anatomical studies: here, however, begins precisely the education, that one understands the living thing to be handled as living, here begins precisely the task of the teachers of education, to suppress there the overall intruding 'historical interest,' where, before all, things must be rightly acted, not recognized. Our mother tongue, however, is a region in which the student must learn to act rightly: and wholly alone according to this practical side is the German lesson necessary in our educational institutions. Of course the historical manner appears to be significantly easier and more comfortable for the teacher; likewise it appears to correspond to a vastly smaller talent, generally a lower flight of his collected willing and striving. But this same perception we will have to make in all fields of pedagogical reality: the easier and the more comfortable wraps itself in the cloak of ostentatious pretensions and of proud titles: the authentically practical, the action belonging to education, as that fundamentally more difficult, earns the glance of ill-will and low esteem: wherefore the honest human being must bring to clarity even this *quid pro quo*[9] to himself and others.

But what is the German teacher now still accustomed to give outside of these scholarly stimuli to a study of the language? How does he connect the spirit of his educational institution with the spirit of the *few* truly educated ones that the German people has, with the spirit of its classical poets and artists? This is a dark and risky domain into which one cannot shed light without terror [Schrecken]: but even here we do not want to hide from ourselves,

9   Latin for "Something for something."

because some time or other everything must become new here. In the Gymnasium the repulsive signature of our aesthetic journalism is being stamped on the still-unformed spirits of the youths: here are being sown by the teacher himself the germs of the raw, willful misunderstanding of our classics, that afterward comports itself as aesthetic criticism and is nothing other than cheeky barbarism. Here the students learn to read of our singular *Schiller* with that boyish superiority, here one accustoms them to smile regarding the noblest and most German of his projects, regarding the Marquis of Posa,[10] regarding Max and Thekla[11] – a smile, regarding which the German genius becomes furious, regarding which a better posterity will blush.

"The last domain in which the German teacher at the Gymnasium is accustomed [pflegt] to be active and which is considered not seldom as the peak of his activity, nay here and there as the peak of Gymnasium education, is the so-called *German work*. For the reason that in this domain almost always the most gifted students bestir themselves with especial desire, one should recognize how precisely dangerously exciting the task assigned here may be. The German work is an appeal to the individual: and the more strongly a student is already conscious of his distinctive qualities, so much more personally will he shape his German work. The 'personal shaping' is, on top of that, already demanded in most of the Gymnasiums through the choice of the themes [Themata]: for which the strongest proof is always, to me, that already in the lower classes one assigns the theme that is in and for itself unpedagogical, through which the student is prevailed upon to give a description of his own life, of his own development. Now one may read through the lists of such themes merely once in a great number of Gymnasiums in order to come to the conviction that probably most of all the students, without their guilt, have to suffer for their lives from this too-early-demanded work of the personality, from this unripe generation of thoughts: and how often the whole later literary

10 A character in Schiller's *Don Carlos*.
11 Characters in Schiller's *Wallenstein* trilogy.

action of a human being appears as the sad result of that pedagogical original sin against the spirit!

"One only has to think what goes before one at such an age with the production of such a work. It is the first production of one's own; the still-undeveloped powers pool together for the first time to a crystallization; the staggering feeling of the required independence clothes these products [Erzeugniße] with a first and foremost, but never returning, captivating magic. All audacities of nature are called forth out of their depths, all vanities, held back by no more powerful barrier, are allowed for the first time to assume a literary form: the young human being feels himself from now on as one who has become ready, as a being capable, indeed required, to speak [Sprechen], to converse [Mitsprechen]. Those themes obligate him to deliver his vote on poets' works or to press together historical persons in the form of a character portrait[12] or independently to present serious ethical problems, or even, with a turned-around light, to illuminate his own becoming and to deliver a critical report on himself: in short, a whole world of the most reflective tasks spreads itself out before the surprised, up-till-now almost unconscious, young human being and is abandoned to his decision.

"Now let us make present [vergegenwärtigen] to us, over against these so-influential first original achievements, the usual activity of the teacher. What appears to him in these works as blameworthy? To what does he make his students attentive? To all excesses of form and thought, that is to everything that in this age is characteristic and individual. The authentic independence that can express itself, at this excitement, all too early in time, only just and wholly alone in awkwardness, in sharpness, and grotesque features, thus precisely the individuality, is reproved and rejected by the teacher in favor of an unoriginal average respectability. On the other hand, uniform mediocrity receives the sullenly distributed praise for precisely with it the teacher is accustomed [pflegt] out of good grounds to be very bored.

12   For an example of Nietzsche's own efforts in this vein, see his character sketch of Cassius in Appendix C.

Lecture II

"Perhaps there are still human beings who see in this complete comedy of German work at the Gymnasium not only the most absurd of all, but also the most dangerous element of all of the present-day Gymnasium. Here originality is desired, but that which is at that age solely possible is in turn rejected: here a formal education is presupposed, to which now generally only the fewest of all human beings come at a ripe age. Here each is considered, without anything further, as a being capable of literature, who is *permitted* to have his own opinions about the most serious things and persons, whereas a correct education [Erziehung] will strive precisely only straight therefrom with all spirit to suppress the laughable claim to independence of judgment and to habituate the young human being to a strict obedience under the scepter of genius. Here a form of presentation in a greater framework is presupposed, at an age in which every spoken or written sentence is a barbarism. Now let us still think in addition of the danger that lies in the lightly excited self-complacency of those years; let us think on the vain feeling with which the youth for the first time sees his literary picture in the mirror – who may, grasping all these effects with *one* glance, doubt therein, that all the defects [Schäden] of our literary-artistic public here will be impressed anew again and again on the generation growing up, the hasty and vain production, the shameful making of books, the perfect lack of style, the unfermented and characterless or lamentably-sprawled out in expression, the loss of any aesthetic canon, the voluptuousness of anarchy and of chaos, in short the literary features of our journalism just as much as of our scholarly community [Gelehrtentums].

"Thereon the fewest know something now, that perhaps among many thousands hardly one is justified to allow himself to be heard as an author, and that *all* others, who attempt it at their danger, earn as their wage for every pressed sentence a Homeric laughter among human beings truly capable of judgment – for it is really a play for gods, to see a literary Hephaestus limp this way, who now indeed wants to offer us something. In this domain, to educate [erziehn] to serious and inexorable habits and views, that is one of the highest tasks of formal education, whereas letting a person have his way in all things of the so-called 'free personality' surely would be nothing other than the recognition mark of barbarism. That, however, at least with the German lesson thought is given not to education, rather to something else, namely to the purported 'free personality,' may have surely become clear out of that which has been reported up till now. And as long as the German Gymnasiums advance in the cultivation [Pflege] of the German work of abominable, conscienceless scribbling, as long as they do not very soon take practical discipline in word and writing as a holy duty, as long as they go around with the mother tongue as if she were only a necessary evil or a dead body, I do not reckon these institutions [Anstalten] among the institutions [Institutionen][13] of true education. Surely one notices least of all, with respect to the language, something of the influence of the *classical model*: wherefore the so-called 'classical education,' which is supposed to emanate from our Gymnasium appears to me from out of this one consideration as something very dubious and leading to misunderstanding. For how could one, with a view to that model, overlook the monstrous seriousness with which the Greek and Roman considered and treated his language from the years of youth on. – how could one fail to recognize his model in such a point, if in others the classical-Hellenic and Roman world really still hovers before the educational plan [Erziehungsplan] of our Gymnasiums as the highest instructing pattern: wherein I at least doubt. Much more it appears, with the claim of the Gymnasium to plant [pflanzen] 'classical education,' only to be a matter of an embarrassed excuse, which then is employed when from any side the capability of the Gymnasium to educate [erzieht] to culture [Bildung] is disputed. Classical education! It sounds so full of dignity! It shames the attacker, it retards the attack – for who is able immediately to see down to the ground of this bewildering formula! And that is the long customary tactic of the Gymnasium: respectively according to the side from out of which the call to battle sounds, it writes upon

13 Nietzsche shifts here, perhaps meaningfully, to a word with Latin roots.

its shield, not precisely decorated with signs of honor, one of those bewildering slogans 'classical education,' 'formal education,' or 'education toward science': three glorious things, which only unfortunately, partly in themselves, partly among one another, are in contradiction and which, if they were forcibly brought together, must bring forth only an educational monster. For a truly 'classical education' is something so unheard of, difficult, and rare and demands so complicated a gift, that it is reserved only for naivete or shamelessness, to promise this as a reachable goal of the Gymnasium. The designation 'formal education' belongs among the raw, unphilosophic phraseology that one must as much as possible beat away: for there is no 'material education.'[14] And whoever puts up the 'education toward science' as the goal of the Gymnasium abandons therewith the 'classical education' and the so-called formal education, generally the whole educational goal of the Gymnasiums for the scientific human being and the educated human being belong to two different spheres, which here and there touch in *one* individual, but never fall together with one another.

"Let us compare these three alleged goals of the Gymnasium with the reality which we observed in the matter of the German lesson; [thus we recognize][15] what these goals mostly are in customary use, flights out of embarrassment, devised for battle and war and really also often enough fit for the deafening of the opponent. For we are able to recognize nothing in the German lesson that reminds us anyhow of the classical-ancient model, of the ancient grandiosity of linguistic education [Erziehung]: formal education however, which is reached through the purported German lesson, proved itself to be the absolute pleasure of the 'free personality,' i.e., as barbarism and anarchy; and what concerns the education [Heranbildung] toward science as a result of that

14   This seems to be a reference to Aristotle's four causes, among which are the formal and the material.

15   "Thus we recognize" is an editors interpolation found in Colli's and Montinari's critical editions. Schlechta's text has exactly the same interpolation.

lesson, our Germanists will have to evaluate with fairness, how little that scholarly beginning of the Gymnasium has contributed to the blood of their science, how much the personality of individual university teachers. – In sum: the Gymnasium neglects up till now the object that is first of all and most near, in which true education begins, the mother tongue: therewith, however, it lacks the naturally fruitful soil for all further educational exertions. For first, on the ground of a rigorous, artistic, careful linguistic discipline and habit [Sitte] the right feeling for the greatness of our classics gains strength, whose recognition on the side of the Gymnasium up till now rests almost solely on the dubious aestheticizing hobbies of individual teachers or on the purely material effect of certain tragedies and novels: one must oneself, however, know from experience, how difficult the language is; one must, after long seeking and wrestling, succeed on the course upon which our great poets stride, in order to feel with them how easily and beautifully they stride upon it and how stiffly or stiltedly the others follow behind them.

"First through such a discipline the young human being receives that physical nausea before the so-beloved and prized 'elegance' of style of our newspaper factory workers and novel writers, before the 'selected diction' of our literary figures and is with one blow and finally elevated above a whole series of right comical questions and scruples, e.g., whether Auerbach[16] or Gutzkow[17] are really poets: one can simply no longer read them for nausea; therewith the question is decided. Let no one believe that it is easy to instruct [auszubilden] his feeling to that physical nausea: but also

16   Berthold Auerbach (1812–1882), author, whose real name was Moyses Baruch, was a member of the Burschenschaft and was associated with the Young Germany movement. He was perhaps most well-known for his *Black Forest Village Stories*.

17   Karl Ferdinand Gutzkow (1811–1878), author, a radical member of the Burschenschaft in his youth and later a leading voice of the Young Germany movement. His literary career alternated between writing dramas and novels and working on journals and periodicals.

let no one hope to come upon one other way to an aesthetic judgment than upon the thorny path of language and indeed not of linguistic research, but of the linguistic self-discipline.

"Here it must thus befall anyone seriously troubling himself like those, as a developing human being, for instance as a soldier is compelled to learn to walk after he was previously a raw dilettante and empiricist in walking. There are troublesome months: one fears that the tendons may tear, one loses all hope that the artistic and consciously learned movements and placements of the feet will ever be performed comfortably and easily: one sees with horror [Schrecken] how clumsily and rawly one puts foot before foot and fears to have unlearned any way of walking and never to learn the right way of walking. And suddenly one notices anew that out of the artistically practiced movements a new habit and second nature is already again come into being, and that the old security and strength [Kraft] of the stride is strengthened and itself turned back with a little grace into the result: now one also knows how difficult the walking is and allows oneself to make fun of the raw empiricists or of the elegant self-begetting dilettantes of walking. Our authors called 'elegant' have, as their style proves, never learned walking: and in our Gymnasiums one does not learn, as our authors prove, to walk. With the right manner of walking of language, however, education begins: which, if it is only begun correctly, afterward also generates against those 'elegant' authors a physical feeling, which one names 'nausea.'

"Here we recognize the fateful consequences of our present day Gymnasium: thereby that it is not in the position to implant [einzupflanzen] the right and rigorous education, which is before all obedience and habituation, thereby that it much more in the best case generally comes to one goal in the excitement and the fructification of scientific drives, explains that so frequently met with alliance of scholarship with barbarism of taste, of science with journalism. One can today in a monstrous universality make the observation [Wahrnehmung] that our scholars have fallen off from and sunken beneath those educational heights that the German system had reached under the exertions [Bemühungen] of Goethe,

Schiller, Lessing,[18] and Winckelmann[19]: a falling off, which shows itself exactly in the gross manner of the misunderstandings to which those men are exposed among us equally well with the historians of literature – whether they are now called Gervinus[20] or Julian Schmidt[21] – as in any company, indeed almost in any conversation among men and women. Mostly, however, and most painfully, this falling off shows itself precisely in the pedagogical literature related to the Gymnasium. It can be attested to [gezeugt] that the sole value that those men have for a true educational institution, for a half century and longer has not once been pronounced not to mention recognized, the value of those men as the preparatory leaders and mystagogues of classical education, in whose hand alone the right way, that leads to antiquity, can be found. Every so-called classical education has only *one* healthy and natural starting point, the artistic, serious, and rigorous habituation in the use of the mother tongue: for this, however, and for the secret of form someone is seldom led from the inside out, out of one's own strength [Kraft] to the right path, while all others need those great leaders and teachers [Lehrmeister] and trust to their keeping. There is, however, indeed no classical education that could grow without this developed [erschlossenen] sense for form. Here where gradually the distinguishing feeling for form and for barbarism awakes, the wing bestirs itself for the first time that carries to the right and sole

18 Gotthold Ephraim Lessing (1729–1781), dramatist and critic, had a powerful influence on German drama and on classical aesthetics. Perhaps his most famous work is *Laokoon*, a study of poetry and of the plastic arts.

19 Johann Joachim Winckelmann (1717–1768), author of a number of highly influential works on classical art (and architecture), an important figure in the development of European classicism.

20 Georg Gottfried Gervinus (1805–1871), university professor and later politician, historian of literature and author, wrote, among other works, a five-volume *History of German Poetry* (originally entitled *History of the Poetical National Literature of the Germans*),

21 Julian Schmidt (1818–1886), literary historian, editor, along with Gustav Freytag of the journal, *Der Grenzbote*.

home of education, to Greek antiquity.[22] Of course we would not come very far with the help of that wing all alone in the attempt to bring ourselves close to that castle of the Hellenic, infinitely distant and enclosed within diamond ramparts: rather anew we need the same leaders, the same teachers, our German classics, in order ourselves to become swept away under the wingbeat of their ancient endeavors – to the land of longing, to Greece.

"Of this sole possible relationship between our classics and classical education, of course, hardly a sound has penetrated into the ancient walls of the Gymnasium. Much more, the philologists have endeavored indefatigably to bring, by their own hand, their Homer and Sophocles to the young souls, and without anything further call the result by an uncontested euphemism 'classical education.' May each himself test in his experience what he has had of Homer and Sophocles at the hand of those indefatigable teachers. Here is a region of the most frequent of all and strongest deceptions and of unintentionally spread misunderstandings. I have still never found in the German Gymnasium even a mere thread that may really call itself 'classical education': and this is not wondrous when one thinks of how the Gymnasium has emancipated itself from the German classics and from the discipline of the German language. With a leap into the blue no one comes into antiquity: and indeed the entire manner how one in the schools traffics with ancient authors, the honest commenting and paraphrasing of our philological teachers is such a leap into the blue.

"Namely, the feeling for the classical-Hellenic is so rare a result of the most strenuous educational struggle and of artistic talent that the Gymnasium can already raise the claim to wake this feeling only through a coarse misunderstanding. In what age? In an age that is still blindly drawn about by the most colorful inclinations of the day, that still carries in itself no notion that that feeling for the Hellenic, *if* it once awoke, immediately becomes aggressive and must express itself in an uninterrupted battle against the alleged culture of the present. For the present-day Gymnasium students

---

22   The wing imagery seems to be a reference to Plato's *Phaedrus*.

the Hellenes as Hellenes are dead: yes, he has his joy in Homer, but a novel by Spielhagen[23] chains him more strongly by far: yes, he swallows Greek tragedy and comedy with relish, but thus a right modern drama, like *The Journalists* by Freitag[24] touches him wholly differently. Yes, he is, with regard to all ancient authors, inclined similarly to read like the art aesthete Hermann Grimm,[25] who once in a tortuous essay on the Venus of Milo[26] finally asks himself: 'What is this form of a goddess to me? What use to me are the thoughts that it can awake in me? Orestes and Oedipus, Iphigenia and Antigone, what do they have in common with my heart?' – No, my Gymnasium students, the Venus of Milo matters nothing to you: but your teachers just as little – and that is the misfortune, that is the secret of the present-day Gymnasium. Who will lead you to the home of education, when your leaders are blind and even still pose as seeing ones! Who of you will come to a true feeling for the holy seriousness of art, if you are methodically [mit Methode] spoiled to stutter independently where one should teach you to speak, to aestheticize independently where one should guide you to be devout before the work of art, to philosophize independently where one should force you to *listen* to great thinkers: all with the

23   Friedrich Spielhagen (1829–1911), a school teacher turned journalist and writer. He produced a large number of novels, novellas, and plays in a relatively short time.

24   *Die Journalisten*, a comedy published by Gustav Freytag [Nietzsche spells the name in German fashion] in 1854. It was first performed on the stage in 1852 and was highly popular and frequently performed for thirty years afterward. It tells the love story of a politically active professor and a colonel's daughter set in a newspaper office. Gustav Freytag (1816–1895) was an author, journalist, and public official. He enjoyed great popular success both with *Die Journalisten* and with his novel *Soll und Haben*, the latter of which praised the merchant class as the solid foundation of the German state.

25   Hermann Grimm (1828–1901), son of Wilhelm Grimm (of fairy-tale fame), in his early days the author of plays and novels, he was in his later years a professor of modern art. He was a noted essayist.

26   The essay is entitled "On the Venus of Milo."

result that you remain eternally distant from antiquity and become servants of the day.

"The most salutary thing which the present-day institution of the Gymnasium contains within itself lies in any case in the seriousness with which the Latin and Greek languages are treated through a whole series of years: here one learns respect for a regularly fixed language, for grammar and lexicon; here one still knows what an error is and will not be incommodated every moment by the claim that even grammatical and orthographical fancies [Grillen] and tricks [Unarten], like in the German style of the present, feel themselves justified. If only this respect for language did not remain hanging thus in the air, as a theoretical burden, so to speak, from which one again immediately unburdens oneself with respect to one's mother tongue! Usually the Greek or Latin teacher accustoms himself with this mother tongue much more to make little of the details; he treats it right from the start as a region in which one may recover again from the rigorous discipline of Latin and Greek, in which the indolent joviality is again allowed with which the German is accustomed to treat everything native [Heimische]. These masterful practices, to translate out of one language into the other, which can fructify in the most salutary thing, even the artistic sense for one's own language, have in the case of German never been conducted with properly categorical rigor and dignity, which here, as with an undisciplined language, needs doing before everything. Of late these practices also disappear evermore: one contents oneself to know the foreign classical languages; one disdains to be proficient in her.

"Here the scholarly tendency in the conception of the Gymnasium breaks through again: a phenomenon, which throws an enlightening light on the education of humanity, which was once taken seriously in an earlier time, as the goal of the Gymnasium. It was the time of our great poets, i.e., those few truly educated [gebildeten] Germans, as from the grandiose Friedrich August Wolf[27] the new classical spirit, streaming from Greece and Rome

27   Friedrich August Wolf (1759–1824), a classical philologist, a highly

through those men, was led into the Gymnasium; his bold beginning succeeded to put up a new image of the Gymnasium that henceforth should become not, so to speak, still merely a nursery of science but before all the authentic shrine for all higher and nobler education.

"From the measures appearing externally necessary thereto, the very essential ones have passed over, with lasting results, into the modern formation of the Gymnasium: only precisely the most important thing did not succeed, to consecrate the teacher himself with this new spirit, so that in the mean time the goal of the Gymnasium has again distanced itself significantly from that education of humanity striven for by Wolf. Much more that old absolute estimate, overcome by Wolf himself, of scholarship and of scholarly education gradually, after a lusterless battle, took the place of the intruding educational principle and maintains now again its exclusive title, if not with the same earlier openness but masked and with a veiled countenance. And that it would not succeed to bring the Gymnasium into the grand train of classical education lay in the un-German, nearly foreign or cosmopolitan, character of these educational endeavors, in the belief that it were possible to draw away the home soil from under the feet and then indeed still be able to stand fast, in the madness that one could spring directly, so to speak, and without bridges, into the alienated Hellenic world through the denial of the German, of the national spirit generally.

"Of course one must first understand how to seek out this German spirit in its hiding under fashionable outer wear or under rubble, one must love it thus in order not to be ashamed even of its atrophied form, one must, before all, guard oneself not to confound it with that which now points to itself with a proud gesture as 'German culture [Kultur] of the present day.' With this that spirit is much more internally at enmity: and precisely in the spheres about

influential and dynamic figure primarily responsible for the creation of modern classical studies in the comprehensive sense. Perhaps his most important work was *Darstellung der Altertumswissenschaft*.

whose lack of culture [Kultur] that 'present day' is accustomed to complain precisely that true German spirit has preserved itself, although not in an apparent [anmuthender] form and under rough exteriors. What, against that, now calls itself, with especial darkness, 'German culture [Kultur]' is a cosmopolitan aggregate which conducts itself toward the German spirit as the journalist toward Schiller, as Meyerbeer[28] toward Beethoven: here the civilization of the French, in the deepest fundamentals un-German, exercises the strongest influence, which is imitated talentlessly and with the most uncertain taste and which in this imitation gives a hypocritical form to German society and press, art and stylistics. Of course it brings this copy nowhere to such an artistically concluded effect which that original civilization, grown forth out of the essence of the Roman, brings forth almost up until our days in France. In order to have a feeling for this contrast, let one compare our most noted German novel writers with any much-less-noted French or Italian writers: on both sides the same dubious tendencies and goals, the same still-dubious means, but there combined with artistic seriousness, at least with linguistic correctness, often with beauty, above all the echo of a corresponding social culture [Kultur]; here everything unoriginal, tottering, in the house coat of thought and of expression or disagreeably spread out, therefore without any background of a real social form, at the highest reminding therein through scholarly manners and knowledge that in Germany the corrupted scholar, in the Roman lands the artistically educated human being becomes a journalist. With this alleged German culture [Kultur], at base unoriginal, the German may promise himself victories nowhere: in it the Frenchman and the Italian shame him and in what concerns the skillful imitation of a foreign culture the Russian before all.

"All the more firmly we hold firm to *the* German spirit, which has revealed itself in the German Reformation and in German

28 Giacomo Meyerbeer (1791–1864), originally Jakob Liebmann Meyer Beer, wrote operas in German, Italian, and French. He was greatly in vogue in Paris in his day and was especially known for spectacular romantic operas. His *L'Africaine* is sometimes still performed today.

music and which has shown that lasting strength, disinclined to all appearance, in the monstrous bravery and rigor of German philosophy and in the of late tested loyalty of the German soldier, from which we may expect even a victory over that fashionable pseudoculture [Pseudokultur] of the 'present day.' The future activity of the school hoped for by us is to draw the true school of education into this battle and especially in the Gymnasium to inflame the new generation growing up for that which is truly German: in which also finally the so-called classical education will again obtain its natural soil and its sole starting point. A true renewal and purification of the Gymnasium will only go forth from a deep and forceful renewal and purification of the German spirit. Very full of secrets and difficult to grasp is the band which is tied between the innermost German essence and the Greek genius. But not before the noblest need of the true German spirit snatches after the hand of this Greek genius like after a firm support in the stream of barbarity, not before a consuming longing after the Greeks breaks forth out of this German spirit, not before the laboriously obtained distant view into the Greek homeland in which Schiller and Goethe restored themselves has become a place of pilgrimage of the best and most gifted human beings will the ideal of classical education, without support, flutter to and fro in the air; and those will at least not be to blame who want to rely upon a still so limited scientificality and scholarship in the Gymnasium in order indeed to have a real, firm, and, for all that, ideal goal in the eye and to save their students in the face of the seductions of that glittering phantom that now lets itself be called 'culture' [Kultur] and 'education' [Bildung]. That is the sad situation of the present day Gymnasium: the most limited standpoints are to a certain measure in the right, because no one is in a position to reach or at least to designate the place where all these standpoints become wrong [Unrecht]." –

– "No one?" The student asked the philosopher with a certain stirring in the voice: and both grew dumb.

LECTURE III

Honored Attendees![1] The conversation, whose listener I once was and whose fundamental features I am attempting here before you to trace from a lively memory, had, at the point where I closed my narration last time, been interrupted by a serious and long pause. The philosopher as well as his companion sat in a gloomy silence sunken there: the just discussed, peculiar situation of need of the most important educational institution, of the Gymnasium, lay upon the soul of each of them as a load for the removal of which the well-meaning individual is too weak and the mass not well-meaning enough. –

Two kinds of things especially grieved our solitary thinkers: at once the clear insight how that which would with right be called 'classical education' now is only an educational ideal floating in the open air,[2] that is not at all able to grow forth out of the soil of our educational apparatus [Erziehungsapparate], however, that, on the contrary, which is now designated by a euphemism, generally accepted and not objected to, as 'classical education,' has only just the value of a pretentious illusion: whose best effect still consists in that the term itself 'classical education' lives indeed still further and has still not lost its pathetic sound. In the German lesson, then, the honorable men had made it clear to one another that previously the right beginning point had up till now not been found for a higher education, raised up on the pillars of antiquity: the wild state of linguistic instruction, the forced entering into scholarly,

1 Nietzsche here addresses the audience as Anwesende, "those present."
2 More literally, "free air."

historical directions in place of a practical discipline and habituation, the knotting together of certain practices, furthered in the Gymnasiums, with the dubious spirit of our journalistic publicity – all these perceptible phenomena in the German lesson gave the sad certainty, that the most salutary forces going out from classical antiquity are still not once suspected in our Gymnasiums, those forces namely, which prepare for battle with the barbarism of the present and which perhaps will once again transform the Gymnasiums into the arsenals and workshops of this battle.

In the mean time it appears on the contrary as if right according to fundamental principles the spirit of antiquity, already on the threshold of the Gymnasium, should be driven away and as if one wanted even here to open the gates as wide as possible to the flattery spoiled system of our present-day, alleged 'German culture' [Kultur]. And if it appears to give a hope for our solitary interlocutors, thus it was the hope that there must be still worse to come, that that, which was previously guessed by few, soon would be penetratingly clear to many, and that then the time of the honorable and of the resolute also for the serious field of the education for the people [Volkserziehung] would no longer be far.

[3]"All the more firmly we hold firm," the philosopher had said," to *the* German spirit which has revealed itself in the German Reformation and in German music and which has shown that lasting strength, disinclined to all appearance, in the monstrous bravery and rigor of German philosophy and in the of-late-tested loyalty of the German soldier, from which we may expect even a victory over that fashionable pseudo-culture [Pseudokultur] of the 'present-day.' The future activity of the school hoped for by us is to draw the true school of education into this battle and especially in the Gymnasium to inflame the new generation growing up for that which is truly German: in which also finally the so-called classical education will again obtain its natural soil and its sole starting point. A true renewal and purification of the Gymnasium will only

3   Here begins a verbatim repetition of the penultimate paragraph of the previous lecture.

go forth from a deep and forceful renewal and purification of the German spirit. Very full of secrets and difficult to grasp is the band which is tied between the innermost German essence and the Greek genius. But not before the noblest need of the true German spirit snatches after the hand of the Greek genius like after a firm support in the stream of barbarity, not before a consuming longing after the Greeks breaks forth out of this German spirit, not before the laboriously obtained distant view into the Greek homeland in which Schiller and Goethe restored themselves has become a place of pilgrimage of the best and most gifted human beings, will the ideal of classical education, without support, flutter to and fro in the air; and those will at least not be to blame who want to rely upon a still-so-limited scientificality and scholarship in the Gymnasium in order to have a real, firm, and, for all that, ideal goal in the eye and to save their students in the face of the seductions of that glittering phantom that now lets itself be called 'culture' [Kultur] and 'education.' [Bildung]"[4]

After some time of silent deliberation the companion turned to the philosopher and said to him: "You wanted to hold out hopes to me, my teacher; but you have increased for me my insight, and thereby my power [Kraft], my courage: really I now look more boldly upon the battlefield, really I already disapprove my all-too-fast flight. We want indeed nothing for us; and even that may not grieve us, how many individuals perish in this battle, and whether we ourselves, for instance, fall among the first. Precisely because we take it seriously, we should not take our poor individuals so seriously; at the moment, where we sink, another will probably grasp the flag in whose signs of honor we believe. I do not even want to reflect about that, whether I am powerful [kräftig] enough for such a battle, whether I will resist long; it may probably even be a death full of honor to fall under the mocking laughter of such enemies, whose seriousness has so frequently appeared to us as something

4   Here ends the repetition and Nietzsche's summary. The last sentence of the repeated paragraph is cut off, as is the philosopher's companion's response.

laughable. I think on the manner how my contemporaries in age prepare themselves for the same calling as I, for the highest calling of the teacher, thus I know how often we laughed precisely about the opposite, and were serious about the most different –"

"Now, my friend," the philosopher interrupted him, laughing, "You speak like one who wants to leap into the water without being able to swim and more than the drowning fears *not* to drown and thereby to become laughed at. Becoming laughed at should, however, be our last fear; for we are here in a sphere where there are so many truths to tell, so many terrifying [erschreckliche], painful, unpardonable truths, that the most upright hatred will not miss us, and rage may merely bring it here and there some time to an embarrassed laughing. Only think for once of unforeseeable hordes of teachers, who have, in the best of faith, taken up into themselves the prevailing educational system [Erziehungssystem], in order now to carry it further with good cheer [Muth's] and without serious deliberating. – As you probably are of the opinion that it must come to this, when they hear of plans on which they are resolved and indeed *beneficies naturae*,[5] of demands which fly out far above their middling capabilities, of hopes which maintain no resonance in them, of battles whose war cry they never once understood and in which they come into consideration only as a dull, resisting, leaden mass. That, however, will probably without exaggeration have to be the necessary position of most of all the teachers in higher educational institutions: indeed whoever considers, how now such a teacher for the most part comes into being, how he *becomes* this teacher of higher education, that one will not once wonder about such a position. There exists now almost all over such an exaggeratedly great number of higher educational institutions that incessantly, endlessly many more teachers are needed for the same than the nature of a people, even with rich aptitudes, is able to beget; and thus an excess of the unfit[6] comes into these institutions, but

5   Latin for "by the benefits of nature," reading *beneficiis* for Nietzsche's *beneficies*.

6   More literally, "the uncalled."

who gradually, through their overwhelming head count and with the instinct of '*similis simili gaudet*,'[7] determine the spirit of those institutions. These may remain only hopelessly distant from pedagogical affairs, who are of the opinion that the manifestly existing surplus [Übertät] in the number of our Gymnasiums and teachers lets itself be transformed through any laws and regulations whatsoever into a real surplus, into an *ubertas ingenii*[8] without a diminution of that number. But about that we must be of one mind, that by nature itself only infinitely rare human beings are destined for a true course of education, and that even a far smaller number of higher educational institutions suffices for their happy development, but that in the present educational institutions, concerned with broad masses, precisely those for whom founding something of such a kind generally first makes sense must feel themselves encouraged least of all.

"The same holds now with regard to the teacher. Precisely the best, those who generally, according to a higher standard, are worthy of this honorable name are now suited, with the present condition [Stande] of the Gymnasium, perhaps least of all to the education [Erziehung] of these unsorted, thrown together youths, but must, to a certain extent, hold secret the best that they could give them; and the monstrous majority of teachers again feel themselves, in the face of these institutions, in the right because their gifts stand in a certain harmonious proportion to the low flight and the inadequacy of their students. From out of this majority resounds that call after ever-new foundings of Gymnasiums and higher teaching institutions: we live in a time, which, through this incessantly resounding call, with a deafening fluctuation, awakens, of all things, the impression, as if a monstrous need in it for education thirsted after satisfaction. But precisely here one must understand how to listen rightly, precisely here one must, unperturbed by the ringing effect of the educational words, look in the face

7   Latin for "like delights in like."
8   Latin for "fullness of nature." The Latin *ubertas* is related by way of pun to the German Übertät.

those who so tirelessly speak of the need for education in their time. Then one will experience a peculiar disillusionment, the same that we, my good friend, have experienced so often: those loud heralds of the need for education suddenly transform themselves, with a serious examination from close up, into zealous, indeed fanatical opponents of true education i.e., that which holds firm to the aristocratic nature of the spirit: for at base they intend as their goal the emancipation of the masses from the mastery of the great individuals, at base they strive after that, to overthrow the holiest order in the empire of the intellect, the servitude of the mass, its submissive obedience, its instinct of loyalty under the scepter of genius.

"I have long accustomed myself thereon to look carefully at all those who speak zealously for the so-called 'education of the people,' as it is commonly understood: for mostly they want for themselves, consciously or unconsciously, with the universal Saturnalia[9] of barbarism, the unfettered [fessellose] freedom which that holy natural order will never grant them; they are born to serving, to obeying, and every moment in which their crawling or wooden-footed or lame-winged thoughts are in action confirms from which clay nature formed them and which trademark she has burned on this clay. Thus education of the mass cannot be our goal: rather education of the individual, selected human beings, equipped for great and lasting works: we know now for once that a just posterity will deliver its judgment on the collective level of education of a people only and completely exclusively according to those great heroes of a time, who walk in solitude, and according to the manner these same were recognized, promoted, honored or made secret, mistreated, destroyed. That which one calls education of the people is to be reached in a direct way, for instance through a universally compulsory elementary instruction, only wholly externally and crudely: the authentic, deeper regions in which the great

9   The Winter solstice festival in ancient Rome. Saturnalia tended to involve merry-making and became increasingly decadent toward the later period of the Roman Empire.

masses generally meet with culture there where the people nour-
ishes its religious instincts, where it further composes in its mythi-
cal images [Bildern], where it keeps up its faith in its custom, its
right, its home soil, its language, all these regions are hardly, and in
any case only through acts of destructive violence, to be reached in
a direct way: and in these most serious things truly to advance education of the people only means so much, to ward off these acts of
destructive violence, and to maintain that wholesome unconsciousness, that sound sleeping of the people, without which counter-
effect, without which remedy no culture [Kultur], with the consuming tension and excitement of its effects, can endure.

"But we know what these strive after who want to disturb that
healing healthy sleep of the people, who want to call continuously
to them: 'Be awake, be conscious! Be clever!' We know where they
aim who pretend to satisfy a powerful educational need, through an
extraordinary increase in all educational institutions, through the
conceited class of teachers engendered thereby. Precisely these
and with precisely these means they fight against the natural order
of rank in the empire of the intellect, they destroy the roots of
those highest and noblest educational forces [Bildungskräfte],
which burst forth out of the unconsciousness of the people, which
have their motherly vocation [Bestimmung] in the begetting of
genius and then in the proper education [Erziehung] and cultivation [Pflege] of the same. Only in the metaphor of the mother will
we conceive the significance and the obligation, which the true
education of a people has in respect to the genius: his own coming
into being does not lie in it; it has, so to speak, only a metaphysical
origin, a metaphysical home. But that it steps into appearance, that
it dives forth from out of the midst of a people, that it, so to speak,
represents the reflected image [Bild], the saturated play of colors of
all the peculiar forces of this people, that it signifies the highest
destiny [Bestimmung] of a people in the metaphorical being of an
individual and in an eternal work, thereby tying up its people in
the eternal and redeeming it from the changing sphere of the
momentary – all that the genius is able to do only if he is ripened
and nourished in the mother's lap of the culture of a people –

whereas, without this sheltering and warming home, he will generally not unfold the wings for his eternal flight, but sadly, with time, like a stranger driven into a wintry desert, slink from there out of the inhospitable land."

"My teacher," the companion said here, "You sit me down in astonishment with this metaphysics of the genius, and only entirely from afar do I divine the correctness of this metaphor. On the other hand I conceive completely what you said about the surplus of Gymnasiums and surplus of higher teachers occasioned thereby; and precisely on this subject I have collected experiences, which testify to me, that the educational tendency of the Gymnasium *must* be directed by this monstrous majority of teachers, who, at bottom, have nothing to do with education and have come to this career and to these titles only through that need. All the human beings, who in a glittering moment of enlightenment [Erleuchtung] have convinced themselves of the singularity and unapproachability of Hellenic antiquity and have defended this conviction before themselves with tiresome struggle. All of these know how the entrance to this enlightenment will never stand open to many and hold it for an absurd, indeed unworthy mode that anyone traffics with the Greeks, so to speak, on account of vocation, for the purpose of earning bread, as with an everyday hand tool, and gropes at these sacred things without awe[10] and with tradesman's hands. But precisely among this class from which the greatest part of Gymnasium teachers are gathered, in the class of the philologists, this crude and irreverent feeling is completely universal: wherefore even now again the propagation[11] and carrying further of such a sentiment into the Gymnasium will not surprise us.

"Let one merely look at the younger generation of philologists; how seldom one notices with them that ashamed feeling that we, with respect to such a world as the Hellenic is, have no right to existence at all. How coolly and audaciously, on the other hand,

10 Scheu could also be translated as "shyness."
11 More literally, "planting forth."

that young brood builds its miserable nests in the midst of the most magnificent temples. The greatest number of them, from their university time onward, wander about so self-satisfied and without shame in the astonishing dreams of the world; a powerful voice should sound out in opposition genuinely from every corner: 'Away from here, you uninitiated, you who will never be initiated, flee silently from this holy place, silently and ashamed!' Oh, this voice sounds out in vain: for one must already be something of the Greek type, in order even merely to understand a Greek curse and formula of banishment! But these are so barbaric that they arrange things comfortably according to their habit among these ruins: they bring along all of their modern conveniences and fancies and, to be sure, they even conceal them behind ancient columns and grave monuments: whereby there is great jubilation when one finds again in an ancient environment what one had first oneself put in earlier with cunning practice. One makes verses and understands enough to consult in the lexicon of Hesychius[12]: immediately he is convinced that he is called to be the adapter of Aeschylus and even finds believers who maintain that he is 'congenial'[13] to Aeschylus, him, the composing wretch [Schmächer]! Again another tracks with the suspicious eye of a policeman all the contradictions, all the shadows of contradictions, that Homer was guilty of making: he squanders his life in tearing apart and putting together Homeric rags, which he himself had first stolen from the lordly garment. A third becomes uneasy near all the mysterious and orgiastic sides of antiquity: he resolves once and for all to allow only the enlightened Apollo to be of value and to see in the Athenian a bright, intelligent, but somewhat immoral Apollonian.[14] How he breathes deep when he had again brought a dark corner of antiquity up to the

12   Hesychius of Alexandria (5th century A.D. ?), compiler of an invaluable lexicon of unusual words and phrases, many drawn from technical languages, older poets, and out of the way dialects.

13   Nietzsche uses the English word here.

14   This use of the term Apollinian seems to be a direct allusion to *The Birth of Tragedy*.

heights of his own enlightenment, when he e.g., has discovered in old Pythagoras an honest comrade in enlightening *politicis.*[15] Another tortures himself with the consideration of why Oedipus should have been condemned by fate to such abominable things as to have to kill his father and marry his mother. Where lies the guilt! Where the poetic justice! Suddenly he knows it: Oedipus had truly been a passionate fellow without all Christian mildness: indeed he even once flew into a wholly unseemly rage – when Tiresias named him a monster and the curse of the whole country.[16] Be sweet tempered! Sophocles wanted perhaps to teach: otherwise you must marry your mother and kill your father! Others, again, their life long count the verses of Greek and Roman poets and delight in the proportion $7:13 = 14:26$.[17] Finally now perhaps one even promises the solution to such a question as the Homeric from the standpoint of prepositions, and believes with ἀνά and κατά[18] to have drawn the truth out of the well. But all, with the most different tendencies, dig and burrow in the Greek soil with a restlessness, a clumsy awkwardness, so that a serious friend of antiquity must become downright anxious: and thus I like to take by the hand any gifted or ungifted human being who has a presentiment of a certain vocational inclination toward antiquity, and perorate [peroriren] before him in the following way: 'Do you even know what kind of dangers threaten you, young one, with a moderate bit of book learning [Schulwissen], on the journey to become a skillful human being? Have you heard that it is an untragic death according to Aristotle to be killed by a statue?[19] And precisely this death threatens you. You wonder at this? Then know that philologists for centuries have attempted to erect again the fallen statues of Greek antiquity that have sunk into the earth, up till now always with insufficient powers:

15 Latin for "in the political."

16 *Oedipus Tyrranus*, line 353.

17 This example may suggest a blending of numerological systems.

18 In Greek, ἀνά means "up" and κατά means "down."

19 *Poetics* 1452a6–9. Aristotle's statement is complicated and bears reading.

for that is a colossus upon which the individuals clamber about like dwarves. A monstrous unified exertion and all the leverage of modern culture [Kultur] are employed: ever again, hardly raised from the soil, it falls back and in the fall smashes the human beings under it. That may even be tolerable: for every being [Wesen] must perish from something: but who guarantees[20] that the statue itself does not break into pieces with this attempt! The philologists perish from the Greeks – that would perhaps be got over – but antiquity itself broken into pieces by the philologist! You consider this, young light-hearted human being, go back, provided you are no iconoclast.'"

"Indeed," said the philosopher, laughing, "there are now numerous philologists, who have gone back as you desire it: and I perceive a great contrast compared to the experiences of my youth. A great horde of them come, consciously or unconsciously, to the conviction that direct contact with classical antiquity is for them useless and hopeless: wherefore even now this study is held by the majority of philologists themselves as sterile, as out-lived, as epigonal. With so much greater pleasure this crowd has thrown itself into the science of language: here, in an endless region of tillable land, freshly opened up, where presently even the most mediocre gifts can be employed with profit and a certain emptiness is already even considered as a positive talent, with the newness and insecurity of the methods and the continuous danger of fantastical errors – here, where work in rank and file is precisely the most desirable thing – here the newcomers are not startled by that cool [abweisende] and majestic voice, which sounds out against them out of the world of the ruins [Trümmerwelt] of antiquity: here one welcomes each one with open arms, and even him, who in the face of Sophocles and Aristophanes was never brought to one unusual impression, to one respectable thought, perhaps with the result that he is placed in an etymological weaver's loom or ordered to engage in the collection of remnants of out-of-the-way dialects – and among combining and separating, collecting and scattering,

20 More literally, "stands for it."

running to and fro and consulting books the day passes him by. But now such a usefully employed language researcher is still supposed to be a teacher before all else! And now he is supposed precisely, according to his duties, to have something to teach about the old authors, for the good of the youth of the Gymnasium, about which he himself has indeed never been brought to impressions, still less to insights! What an embarrassment! Antiquity says nothing to him, and as a result he has nothing to say about antiquity. Suddenly it becomes clear to him:[21] for what reason is he a scholar of language! Why did those authors write Greek and Latin! And now he cheerfully begins at once to etymologize with Homer and uses Lithuanian or Church Slavonic, but before all holy Sanskrit for help, as if the Greek lessons were only an excuse for a general introduction into the study of language and as if Homer suffered from only one principal defect, namely, not having been written in Ur-Indogermanic. Whoever is familiar with the present Gymnasiums, he knows how very estranged their teachers are from the classical inclination [Tendenz],[22] and how precisely out of a feeling of this defect those scholarly occupations with comparative language science have thus increased."

"I am of the opinion," said the companion, "it would be precisely the point that a teacher of classical education just does *not* mix up his Greeks and Romans with the others, with the barbaric peoples, and that for him Greek and Latin could *never* be one language *alongside* others; precisely for his classical inclination [Tendenz] it is indifferent whether the skeleton of this language should agree with or be related to that of other languages: the agreement is not the point for him: precisely to that *which is not common*, precisely to that which places those peoples above all other peoples as not barbaric, adheres his real interest [Teilnahme], exactly insofar as he is a teacher of culture [Bildung] and wants to remodel [umbilden] himself on the elevated model of the classics."

"And I may be deceiving myself," said the philosopher, "But I

21 More literally, "Suddenly it becomes clear and well."
22 Tendenz is translated elsewhere as "tendency."

have the suspicion that with the manner that Latin and Greek are taught now in the Gymnasiums, precisely the ability, the mastery over the language that allowed one to express oneself comfortably in speaking and writing has gone lost: something wherein my generation, now of course already become very aged and scarce, distinguished itself: whereas to me the present-day teachers seem to go around with their students so genetically and historically that finally in the best case they also become from that little Sanskritists or little etymological spitting devils or conjecturing libertines, but none of them can read his Plato, his Tacitus, with delight like us old ones. Thus the Gymnasiums may even now still be nurseries [Pflanzstätten] of scholarship, but not of the scholarship, which, so to speak, is only the natural and unintentional side-effect of an education directed by the noblest goals, rather much more of that, which might be compared with the hypertropic swelling of an unhealthy body. For this scholarly obesity the Gymnasiums are nurseries: if they have not indeed degenerated into wrestling schools for the elegant barbarism that now is accustomed to boast of itself as 'German culture of the present time.'"

– "But to where," answered the companion, "should those poor countless teachers flee, on whom nature bestowed no dowry [Mitgift] of true education, who have come to put forward the title [Anspruch] teacher [Bildungslehrer] much more through a necessity, because the excess of schools requires an excess of teachers, and in order to nourish themselves! To where should they flee, if antiquity authoritatively rejects them! Must they not fall as sacrifices to those powers of the present, who day by day call to them from the tirelessly ringing organ of the press: 'We are culture [Kultur]! We are education [Bildung]! We are the heights! We are the peak of the pyramid! We are the goal of world history!' – when they have the seductive promises, when precisely the most shameful signs of non-culture [Unkultur], the plebian publicity of the so-called 'interests of culture' [Kulturinteressen] in the journal and the newspaper, are extolled to them as the foundation of a wholly new, highest of all, ripest form of education! To where should the poor ones flee, when in them also just a residue of a notion lives that those promises may be very deceitful – to where other than into the most stunted,[23] micrologically most sterile scientificality, merely in order here no longer to hear the untiring shouting about education? Must they not, proceeding in this manner, finally, like an ostrich, stick their head in a pile of sand! Is it not true luck [Glück][24] for them that, buried among dialectics, etymologies, and conjectures, they lead an ant life, even if at a miles-wide distance from true education, thus at least with the ears plastered over and deaf and sealed against the voice of the elegant culture of the time [Zeitkultur]?"

– "You are right, my friend," said the philosopher: "but where lies that brazen necessity that an excess of schools [Bildungs-schulen] must exist and that through them again an excess of teachers [Bildungslehrern] becomes necessary? – when we indeed so clearly recognize that the demand for this excess sounds out of one of the spheres that is an enemy of culture [Bildung] and that the consequences of this excess also only benefit[25] non-culture [Unbildung]? Indeed the discourse can be of such a brazen necessity only insofar as the modern state is accustomed in these things to take part in the discussion and is wont to accompany its demands with a blow in its defense [Rüstung]: which phenomenon then certainly makes the same impression in most, as if the eternal brazen necessity, the original law of things speaks to them. Speaking with such demands, a 'culture state' [Kulturstaat], as one now says, is for the rest something young and has first become a 'matter of self-evidence' in the last half-century, i.e., in a time in which, according to its favorite phrase, so many kinds of 'self-evident' appear, which in themselves are out and out not evident to themselves.[26] Precisely by the most powerful modern state, by Prussia, this right to the highest leadership in education and school has been taken so

23 More literally, stumpfeste means "most stumpy." Stumpfen is translated as "stupid" in the quotation from Goethe's *Epilogue to the Bell* in Nietzsche's Introduction.

24 Glück could also be translated as "happiness."

25 More literally, "come to good."

26 More literally, "not evident by themselves."

seriously, that, with the boldness that is characteristic of this political system, the dubious principle adopted by it receives a significance understood as universally threatening and dangerous for the true German spirit. For from out of this side we find the striving to bring the Gymnasium up to the so-called 'height of the time' formally systematized: here bloom all those preparations through which as many students as possible are spurred on to a Gymnasium education [Gymnasialerziehung]: here the state even has employed its most powerful means of all, the granting of certain privileges relating to military service, with the result that, according to the impartial testimony of statistical officials, precisely from this and only from this the universal congestion of all Prussian Gymnasiums and the most urgent, persistent demand for new institutions [Gründungen] is to be explained. What more can the state do in favor of an excess of educational institutions than if it brings all the higher and the greatest part of the lower civil-servant positions, attendance at a university, even the most influential military privileges into a necessary connection with the Gymnasium. And this in a country, where the universal, thoroughly popularly approved, military service just as well as the unlimited, political ambition for civil offices unconsciously draws all gifted natures toward these directions. Here the Gymnasium above all is viewed as a certain rung on the ladder of honor: and everything that feels a drive toward the sphere of government will be found on the course of the Gymnasium. This is a new and, in each case, original phenomenon [Erscheinung][27]: the state presents itself as a mystagogue of culture [Kultur] and while it advances its purposes, it compels each of its servants to appear[28] before it only with the torch of universal state education in their hands: in whose restless light they are supposed to recognize again it itself as the highest goal, as the reward of all their educational exertions. Now the last phenomenon

---

27 The word translated here and soon below as "phenomenon" was the Latinate cognate "Phänomen." Erscheinung could be translated more simply as "appearance."

28 The verb here is "erscheinen."

[Phänomen] should indeed make them surprised: it should remind, e.g., of that related, gradually conceived tendency of a philosophy, which was freely advanced for the sake of the state and which was aiming at the purposes of the state, of the tendency of the Hegelian philosophy: yes, it would perhaps not overstate to maintain that in the subordination of all educational endeavors under the purposes of the state Prussia has appropriated the practical, usable heirloom of the Hegelian philosophy with success: whose apotheosis of the state in all things reaches its peak in *this* subordination."

– "But," asked the companion, "what kind of intentions may the state pursue in such a strange tendency? For that it pursues intentions of the state already follows, as those conditions of the Prussian schools are marveled at by other states, carefully weighed, here and there imitated. These other states obviously suppose here something that could be of use for the duration and power of the state in a similar way, so to speak, as that universal military service which is famous and becoming thoroughly popular. There where everyone periodically and with pride wears the soldier's uniform, where almost everyone has absorbed into themselves the uniform state culture [Staatskultur] through the Gymnasium, overexuber-ant ones [Überschwängliche] may almost speak of ancient condi-tions, of an omnipotence of the state one time reached only in antiquity, which almost every young human being, by instinct and education [Erziehung] continues to feel as the flower and highest purpose of human existence." –

"This comparison," said the philosopher, "would now certain-ly be overexuberant [überschwänglich] and would not limp only on *one* leg. For precisely the essence of the ancient state remained as far as possible from this utilitarian consideration, which only holds valid culture as far as it is directly of use to it and which probably even wishes to annihilate the drives which do not immediately prove applicable to its intentions. The profound[29] Greek felt pre-cisely therefore toward the state the strong feeling, for the modern

29 Tiefsinnige might also be translated as "deep thinking" or "deep feeling."

human being almost offensive, of admiration and thankfulness, because he recognized that without such an institution for distress[30] and protection not even a single germ of culture [Kultur] could develop, and that his wholly inimitable and for all times singular culture [Kultur] grew up so luxuriantly precisely under the careful and wise guard [Obhut] of *its* institutions for distress and protection. The state was not a border guard, regulator, or overseer for his culture; rather the robust, muscular comrade, ready for battle, and companion on the way, who gives the admired, nobler, and, as it were, unearthly [überirdischen] friend safe conduct through the harsh realities and for that earns his thankfulness. If now on the contrary the modern state lays claim to such an enthusiastic thankfulness, thus this certainly does not happen because it was itself conscious of chivalrous service to the highest German culture and art: for on this side its past is just as disgraceful as its present: whereby one has only to think of the manner [Art] and way [Weise] that the memory of our greatest poets and artists is celebrated in major German cities, and how the highest artistic plans of these German masters have ever been supported on the side of this state.

"It must thus be a matter apart,[31] as well with that tendency of the state which promotes in all ways that which is here called 'education,' as with that thus promoted culture [Kultur] which subordinates itself to this tendency of the state. With the genuine [echten] German spirit and an education deriving from it, as I sketched it out to you, my friend, with gradual strokes, that tendency of the state finds itself in open or hidden feud: *the* spirit of education, which does well with that tendency of the state and is supported by it with such lively interest [Teilnahme],[32] according to which its school system is admired in foreign countries, must according to that probably originate from a sphere which never comes into contact with that genuine German spirit, with that spirit which speaks

---

30 Not is more usually translated as "necessity" or "need."

31 More literally, "it must thus have its own explanation," or "it must thus have its own reason."

32 Teilnahme could also be translated as "participation.'

to us so wondrously out of the innermost kernel of the German Reformation, of German music, of German philosophy, and which, like a noble exile, precisely is viewed so indifferently, so contemptuously by that education thriving[33] due to the state. It is a stranger: in solitary sorrow it marches past: and there the censer is swung before that pseudo-culture [Pseudokultur], which, amid that acclaim of the 'educated' [gebildeten] teacher and newspaper writer, arrogates to itself *its* titles, its honors, and with the term 'German' works a disgraceful game. Whereto does the state need that surplus of educational institutions, of teachers? Whereto this education of the people, grounded on breadth, and this enlightenment of the people? Because the genuine German spirit is hated, because one fears the aristocratic nature of true education, because one wants to drive the great individuals thereby into self-imposed exile, so that one may plant and nurture pretensions to education in the many, because one seeks therewith to run away from the narrow and hard discipline of great leaders, so that one may persuade the mass it will find the way even by itself – under the guiding star of the state! A new phenomenon! The state as the guiding star of education! In the mean time one thing consoles me: this German spirit which one thus fights, for which one has substituted a colorfully adorned vicar, the spirit is brave: it will thoroughly save itself fighting into a purer period, it will, noble, as it is, and victorious, as it will be, preserve in itself a certain sympathetic feeling toward the state system, when this, in its need and hard pressed at the extreme, grasped such a pseudo-culture [Pseudokultur] as an ally. For what does one know finally of the difficulty of the task of governing human beings, i.e., to preserve upright law, order, quiet, and peace among many millions of a species in which the great majority are boundlessly egoistic, unjust, unfair, dishonest, envious, wicked, and thereby very limited and queer in the head, and thereby continually to protect the little which the state itself acquires as a possession, against greedy neighbors and malicious robbers? Such a hard pressed state grasps after any ally: and if

33   More literally, "luxuriating."

indeed one such offers itself in pompous turns of phrase, if he designates it, the state, for example, as this Hegel did, as the 'absolutely complete ethical organism'[34] and presents as the task of education for each to find out the place and position where he can be of most useful service to the state – who will take it as a wonder, when the state without further ado falls upon the neck of such an ally offering itself and now even with its deep barbaric voice and full conviction calls to it: 'Yes! You are education! You are culture [Kultur]!'"– –

34 I have not found this exact phrase anywhere in Hegel. But most readers of *The Philosophy of Right* would grant Nietzsche to be in the right in ascribing this thought to Hegel.

LECTURE IV

My honored listeners! After you have truly followed my story up to this point and in common we have overcome that solitary, remote, here-and-there offending dialogue of the philosopher and his companion, I must hold out hope to myself that you, even now, like robust swimmers, have the desire to endure the second half of our journey, especially since I can promise you that now a few other puppets will show themselves on the little marionette theater of my experience and that generally, in case you have up to this point persevered, the waves of the story shall carry you now more easily and quickly to the end. Namely, we have now almost arrived at a turning point: and it should be ever so advisable to secure ourselves once again, with a short look back, at that which we think to have gained from such an exchange rich conversation.

"Remain at your post," thus the philosopher appeared to call to his companion: "for you may cherish hopes. For ever more clearly it shows itself that we have no educational institutions, but that we must have them. Our Gymnasiums, their structure pre-established according to this elevated purpose, have become either the nurseries [Pflegestätten] of a dubious culture [Kultur], which defends itself with deep hatred from a true, i.e., aristocratic education based upon a wise selection of spirits: or they raise [ziehen] up a micrological, sterile scholarship, in any case remaining far from education, whose value consists perhaps precisely therein, at least to make the eye and ear dull in the face of the seduction of that questionable culture [Kultur]." The philosopher has before all made his companion attentive to the strange degeneration that must have entered into the kernel of a culture [Kultur] when the state is permitted to believe it rules over it, when the state reaches state goals through culture, when the state, combined with culture, battles against other hostile powers as well as against the spirit that the philosopher dared to name the "true German spirit." This spirit, chained to the Greeks through the noblest need, proven in a difficult past as persevering and courageous, pure and sublime[1] in its goals, made capable by its art for the highest task, to redeem modern human beings from the curse of the modern – this spirit is condemned, apart, to live estranged from its heritage: but if its slow lament sounds through the waste of the present, then the glutted and colorfully adorned caravan of education of the present is horrified [erschrickt]. Not only wonder [Erstaunen], but horror [Schrecken], should we bring. That was the opinion of the philosopher, not to flee shyly therefrom; rather to attack was his advice: but especially he exhorted his companion not to think too anxiously and carefully on the individual out of whom, through a higher instinct, the inclination against the present barbarity streams. "Let it perish: the Pythian god was not at a loss to find a new tripod, a second Pythia, so long anyhow as the mystic vapor still sprang from the deep."[2]

Anew the philosopher raised his voice: "Note it well, my friend," he said, "two sorts of things you may not confuse. A human being must learn very much in order to lie, in order to fight his fight for existence: but everything that he learns and does in this respect as an individual still has nothing to do with education. This begins, on the contrary, first in a stratum that hangs high above that world of necessity, of the struggle for existence, of neediness. It is now a question how much a human being esteems his subject next to other subjects, how much of his power he uses up for that individual life struggle. Many a one, by a Stoic-narrow limitation of his

1   Or "elevated."

2   The Pythian god is Phoebus Apollo. This designation identifies Apollo as the god of the oracle at Dephi. The oracle, called the Pythia, made her predictions while seated upon a tripod placed over a fissure in the earth that emitted vapors. The reference to finding a new tripod may refer to the varying myths according to which Hercules stole the tripod.

requirements, will very soon and easily elevate himself in that sphere, in which he may forget and, as it were, shake off his subject, in order now to enjoy eternal youth in a solar system of timeless and impersonal matters. Another extends so in width the effect and the requirements of his subject and builds in such an astonishing measure the mausoleum of this his subject, as if he were thus in a position to overcome in wrestling the monstrous opponent, time. Even in such a drive the longing after immortality shows itself: riches and power, cleverness, presence of mind [Geistesgegenwart], eloquence, a blooming aspect, an important name – everything has become here only a means with which the insatiable personal will to life longs after new life, with which it thirsts after a finally illusory eternity.

"But even in this highest form of the subject, even in the most heightened requirement of such an extended and, as it were, collective individual, there is still no touching on true education: and when from out of this side, e.g., art is longed after, thus come into consideration precisely only the dissipating or stimulating aspects of its effects, thus those which understand how to inspire pure and elevating art least and degraded and polluted art best. For in his collected doings and strivings, as grandiose as he may perhaps look to the observer, he was indeed never free from his desiring and restless subject: that illuminated, ethereal sphere of subject-free contemplation flees back before him – and therefore, though he may learn, travel, collect, he must live banished and in an eternal distance from true education. For true education disdains polluting itself with the needing and desiring individual: it knows how wisely to give the slip to those, who would like to secure it as a means for egoistic aims; and if even one person fancies himself to hold it fast, in order now perhaps to make a living [Erwerb][3] out of it and to satisfy his necessities of life through its exploitation, then it runs away suddenly with inaudible steps and with a mien of derision.

"Thus my friend, do not confuse this education, this dainty-footed, fastidious, ethereal goddess, with that useful maid which

3   Erwerb is translated elsewhere as "acquisition" or "earnings."

occasionally is also named 'education,' but is only the intellectual servant and advisor of the necessities of life, of earnings [Erwerb], of neediness. But that education [Erziehung], which at the end of its course holds out the prospect of an office or bread-winning, is no education [Erziehung] toward culture [Bildung], as we understand it; rather it is only an instruction [Anweisung] in what ways one can save and protect his subject in the struggle for existence. Certainly such an instruction is for most human beings of first and second [nächster][4] importance; and the harder the struggle is, the more the young human being must learn, the more he must strain every nerve to make his powers felt.

"But let no one believe that these institutions that spur him on and make him capable for this struggle could in any way come to be considered in a serious sense as cultural institutions. They are institutions for the overcoming of the necessities of life, whether they promise now to produce [bilden] civil servants or merchants or officers or wholesalers or farmers or doctors or technicians. But for such institutions in any case different kinds of laws and rules apply than for the erection of a cultural institution: and what is allowed here, indeed offered as much as possible, may be a sacrilegious injustice there.

"I want to give you an example, my friend. If you want to lead a young human being on the right cultural path [Bildungspfad], thus guard well against disturbing the naïve, trusting, at the same time personally-immediate relationship of the same to nature: to him must the forest and the rock, the storm, the vulture, the individual flower, the butterfly, the meadow, the mountain slope speak in their own tongues; in them must he at some time recognize himself again as in countless dispersed [auseinandergeworfen] reflections and mirages [Spiegelhagen], in a colorful whirl of changing appearances; thus will he unconsciously have a feeling for the metaphysical oneness of all things in the great likeness of nature and at the same time calm himself in its eternal persistence and necessity. But how many young human beings should be allowed

4   More literally, "next."

to grow up placed so near and almost personally close to nature! The others must at an early time learn a different truth: how one places nature under one's yoke. Here that naïve metaphysics is at an end: and physiology of plants and animals, geology, inorganic chemistry compel their followers toward a completely altered consideration of nature. What has been lost through this new compulsory kind of consideration is not, let us say, a poetic phantasmagoria, rather the instinctive, true, and singular understanding of nature, in whose place a clever calculation and outwitting of nature now has tread. Thus is granted to the truly cultured [Gebildeten] the inestimable good of being able to remain true to the contemplative[5] instincts of their childhood without any break and through that to come to a rest, unity, to a togetherness and harmony, which cannot be suspected even once by one drawn into the struggle for life.

"Indeed do not believe thus, my friend, that I wish to starve our Realschulen and higher Bürgerschulen[6] of their praise: I honor the places in which one learns to calculate in an orderly fashion, where one takes possession of the languages of commerce, takes geography seriously and arms oneself with the astonishing findings of natural science. I am also ready and willing to add that those prepared at the better Realschulen of our day are completely entitled to the pretensions which the accomplished Gymnasium students are accustomed to make, and the time is certainly no longer distant where one will find universities and state offices in general just so unlimitedly open to students of such a kind as hitherto only to the students of the Gymnasium – mark well, to the students of the present Gymnasium! But I cannot suppress this painful concluding sentence: if it is true, that the Realschule and the Gymnasium in their present goals in whole are so much of one mind and only deviate from one another in such slight ways [7] as to be able to be reckoned of completely equal status before the forum of the state –

5   Here the German is "beschaulich"; earlier "Contemplation" was translated as contemplation.

6   Bürgerschulen are higher elementary schools.

thus we lack therewith one species of educational institutions [Erziehungsanstalten] completely: the species of cultural institutions [Bildungsanstalten]! This is in the least a reproach against the Realschulen, which have up till now followed many low, but highly necessary, tendencies ever so happily as honestly; but much less honestly it goes into the sphere of the Gymnasium, also much less happily: for here lives something of an instinctive feeling of shame, from an unconscious recognition that the whole institution is disgracefully degraded and that the sonorous, cultured words of clever, apologetic teachers contradict the barbaric-desolate and sterile reality. Thus there are no cultural institutions [Bildungsanstalten]! And there, where one at least still feigns their miens, one is more hopeless, more emaciated, more dissatisfied than in the herds of the so-called 'realism'! Besides, note, my friend, how raw and uninformed one must be in the society of teachers, if one could misunderstand the rigorous philosophical terms 'real' and 'realism' to such a degree as to suspect behind them the opposition of matter and spirit, as to be able to interpret 'realism' as the 'route to knowledge, formation, mastery of the actual.' –

"For my part, I know only one true opposition: *Institutions of Culture* [Bildung] and *Institutions for the Necessities of Life*: to the second genus belong all those ready to hand, but I am speaking of the first." –

Perhaps two hours may have gone by, during which both philosophical companions conversed about such surprising things. In the mean time it had become night: and if already in the twilight the voice of the philosopher had resounded like a natural music in the forested enclosure, in the complete black of night, when he spoke excitedly or even passionately, the sound now broke forth in manifold thunderings, crackings, and hissings, losing itself in the tree trunks and boulders down in the valley. Suddenly he became silent: he had just repeated with an almost piteous expression, "We have no cultural institutions. We have no cultural institutions." – There something, perhaps a fir cone, fell immediately down in

7   More literally, "lines."

front of him. Barking, the dog of the philosopher rushed up to this something: – thus interrupted, the philosopher raised his head and felt all at once the night, the cool, the loneliness. "Well, what are we doing!" he said to his companion: "It has indeed become dark. You know whom we are awaiting here: but he is no longer coming. We were here so long for nothing: we should go."

Now I must make you familiar, my honored listeners, with the sensations with which I and my friend, from out of our hiding-place, had followed the clearly perceived and, by us, greedily over-heard conversation. I have indeed told you that we, at that place and at that hour of the evening, had intended to celebrate a festival of remembrance: this remembrance was connected with nothing other than cultural- [Bildungs-] and educational- [Erziehungs-] things of which we, after our youthful belief, had brought home a rich and happy harvest out of our previous life. Thus we were then especially inclined, to remember with thanks the institution, which we once, in this place, had contrived so that, as I already earlier intimated, mutually to spur on and watch over our living cultural impulses [Bildungsregungen] in a small circle of companions. But suddenly a wholly unexpected light fell upon that whole past, as we silently and attentively[8] abandoned ourselves to the strong speeches of the philosopher. We came before ourselves, like such, who all at once in unwatchful wandering find their foot on an abyss: we seemed not only to have missed the great danger but to have run to meet it. Here, in the place so memorable for us, we heard the warning: "Back! No step further! Do you know whereto your feet carry you, whereto this gleaming path entices you?" –

It seemed that we knew it now, and a feeling of overflowing thanks led us thus irresistibly to the serious warner and the loyal Eckart,[9] that we both, at the same time, sprang up so as to embrace the philosopher. This one was just on the point of leaving and had already turned sideways; as we thus unexpectedly, with loud steps,

8   Lauschend could also be translated "eavesdropping." "Lauschte" is translated as "eavesdropped" in Lecture I.

9   The references to the warner and to the loyal Eckart seem to be to

sprang up to him, and the dog with sharp barking threw itself in opposition to us, he, together with his companion, was more inclined to think it a robbery than an inspired embrace. Clearly he had forgotten us. Put briefly, he ran from there. Our embrace miscarried completely, as we overtook him. For my friend shrieked at that moment because the dog had bitten him, and the companion pounced on me with such weight that we both collapsed. There arose, between the dog and the man, an uncanny activity on the soil which lasted a few moments – until my friend succeeded in calling with a strong voice, and parodying the words of the philosopher: "In the name of all culture [Kultur] and pseudo-culture [Pseudokultur]! What does the stupid dog want from us! Cursed dog, away from here you uninitiated, never to be initiated, away from us and our guts [Eingeweiden], go back silent, silent and ashamed!"

After this address the scene clarified itself somewhat: as far as it could be clarified in the complete darkness of the forest. "It is you!" called the philosopher. "Our pistol shooters! How you terrified us! What drives you so to rush upon me at night time?"

– "Joy, thanks, reverence drive us," we said and shook the hand of the gray one [Greis], during which the dog discharged a barking rich with presentiment. "We don't want to let you go without saying this to you. And so as to be able to explain everything to you, you must also still not go forth: we still want to ask you also about so many things[10] that we have on our hearts just now! Now you remain: every step of the way is familiar to us; we can conduct you down afterward. Perhaps even the guest awaited by you will still come. Look now there below at the Rhine: what swims there so

the same man. "Loyal Eckart" is a figure from the hero sagas. Ludwig Tieck's *Der Getreue Eckart und der Tannenhaüser* (*Loyal Eckart and the Tannhaüser*, 1799) portrays the knight Eckart both as a warner and as an old grey one [Greis]. In Tieck's story, which was likely one of the sources for Wagner's opera *Tannhaüser*, Eckart was placed before the Venusberg (the mountain of the love goddess) to warn men of its dangers.

10 The German text places the exclamation mark in the middle of the

bright, as under the blaze of many torches about it? There in the middle of the torches I will seek your friend; indeed I already have a presentiment that he will come up to you with all these torches."

And so we assailed the amazed gray one with our requests, our promises, our fantastical delusions, until finally even the companion tried to persuade the philosopher still to go up and down somewhat here on the heights of the mountain in the mild night air, "unburdened by all smoky knowledge [Wissenqualm],"[11] as he added.

"Oh, shame on you!" said the philosopher, "indeed you are in a position, when for once you wish to cite something, to cite nothing but Faust. Yet, I wish to give in to you, with or without the citation, if only our young ones hold still and do not run away just as suddenly as they arrived: for they are like will-o'-the-wisps; one is amazed when they are there and again when they are no longer there."

Here my friend recited immediately:

"Out of reverence, I hope, should we succeed,
to compel the easy-going nature.
Our course usually goes only zig-zag."[12]

The philosopher was amazed and remained standing still. "You surprise me," he said. "My Masters Will-o'-the Wisps: this is indeed no swamp! What is this place for you? What does the proximity of a philosopher signify to you? There the air is sharp and clear, there the soil is dry and hard. You ought to seek out a fantastical region for zig-zagging inclinations."

"I think," the companion spoke here in between, "The Masters have already told us, that a promise binds them for this hour in this place: but as it appears to me they have also, belonged

sentence after "many things" and may indicate a particular emphasis on "many."

11 The companion quotes from *Faust* I, 395.

12 Nietzsche's friend not only quotes from *Faust* (I, 3860–3862), but he quotes the speech of a will-o'-the-wisp that is acting as a guide.

to our comedy about education [Bildungskomoedie] as the chorus, and indeed as truly 'Ideal Spectators'[13] – for they have not disturbed us, we believed ourselves to be alone with one another."

"Yes," said the philosopher, "that is true: this praise may not be denied them, but it seems to me that they deserve a still greater –"

Here I seized the hand of the philosopher and said, "That one must indeed be stupid [stumpf] like a reptile, belly in the dirt, head in mud, who could listen to such a speech as yours without becoming serious and reflective, indeed excited and hot. Perhaps someone or another would become angry thereby, out of vexation and self-accusation; but with us the impression was otherwise, only that I do not know how I should describe it. Precisely this hour was so selected for us, our mood was so prepared, we sat there like open vessels – now it appears that we have been overfilled with this new wisdom, for I do not know how to help myself any more, and if anyone asked me what I want to do tomorrow or what I generally have resolved myself to do from now on, thus I would not know at all how to answer. For clearly we have up till now lived wholly otherwise, we have educated [gebildet] ourselves wholly otherwise than is right – but what do we do, in order to get over the chasm of today to tomorrow."

"Yes," confirmed my friend, "So goes it with me as well, thus I ask likewise: but then to me it is as if I generally, through such high and ideal views of the task of German education, was frightened away from it, yes, as if I were not worthy to participate[14] in its achievement. I see only a gleaming train of the richest natures of all moving themselves toward that goal; I have a notion over which abysses, into which temptation this train drives. Who can be so bold, to join this train?"

Here the companion also turned again to the philosopher and

13   The doctrine of regarding the chorus as ideal spectators derives from August Wilhelm Schlegel, (1767–1845), *Lectures on Dramatic Art and Literature*, Lecture V. See Nietzsche's discussion of this doctrine in section seven of *The Birth of Tragedy*.

14   More literally, "to build with."

said: "Do not blame me also, if I feel something similar and if I now express it before you. In the conversation with you it often happened to me thus, that I felt raised up above myself and I warmed myself in your courage, your hopes to the point of self-forgetting. Then came a cooler moment; some sharp wind of reality brought me to reflection – and then I see only the wide chasm ripped open between us, over which you yourself carried me away, as in a dream. What you call education, that dangles around me then or presses hard upon my breast, that is a coat of mail by which I am pressed down, a sword that I cannot swing."

Suddenly, in the face of the philosopher, we three were of one mind and reciprocally stimulating and encouraging each other we jointly brought forth approximately the following, while we slowly walked up and down with the philosopher on the treeless plain, which had served us on that day as a shooting range, in the completely silent night and under a calmly outstretched, starry sky.[15]

"You have spoken so much of the genius," we said, or thereabouts, "of his solitary, difficult journey through the world, as if nature only produced the most extreme opposites, at one time the stupid [stumpfe], sleeping, instinctually proliferating masses and then at a monstrous distance therefrom the great, contemplative individuals, equipped for eternal creations. But now you call those same the pinnacles of the intellectual pyramid: yet it seems that, from the broad, heavily encumbered foundation up to the free, towering peaks countless intermediary degrees are necessary, and that precisely here the principle must hold: *natura non facit saltus*.[16] But where now begins what you call education, at which freestone [Quadern][17] do the spheres divide that are ruled from beneath and

15 Nietzsche's text does not start a new paragraph here.
16 Latin for "nature makes no leaps." Cf. *Schopenhauer as Educator*, section 5; *KSA* 1.380.18, where Nietzsche repeats this principle in German but then suggests a qualification or exception. Cf. *The Wanderer and His Shadow*, section 198.
17 A freestone is a stone that may be cut freely without splitting. It is a kind of natural articulation.

the others from above? And if one may only speak truly of 'education' with respect to these most remote natures, how will one ground institutions on the incalculable existence of such natures, how may one reflect about educational institutions that only come to good for just those chosen few? Much more it appears to us that precisely these ones know how to find their way and that therein their strength shows itself to be able to walk without such educational crutches as everyone else and thus, undisturbed, to stride through the pressing and pushing of world history, almost like a ghost through a great, closely packed assembly."

Something of this kind we brought forth with one another, without much skill [Geschick] and order; indeed the companion of the philosopher went still further and said to his teacher, "Now you yourself think on all the great geniuses, upon which we precisely are accustomed to be proud of as genuine [ächte] and true leaders and guides of that true, German spirit, whose memory we honor through festivals and statues, whose works we hold up against foreign lands with self-confidence: wherein in these ones is such an education, as you demand for them, encountered [entgegenkommen], how far do they show themselves nourished and ripened by the sun of a native education? And despite that they have been possible, and despite that they have become what we now have to reverence. Indeed their works justify perhaps precisely the form of development that these noble natures took, indeed perhaps they justify even such a defect in education that we must probably concede to their time and to their people. What did Lessing, what did Winckelmann take from a contemporary German education? Nothing, or at least just so little as Beethoven, as Schiller, as Goethe, as all of our great artists and poets. Perhaps it is a natural law, that always only the later generations must become conscious of the heavenly gifts through which an earlier generation had become excellent."

Here the philosophic graybeard flew into a vehement rage and shouted at his companion: "Oh you lamb in innocence of experience! Oh you, all of you, nursing animals, to be giving you a name! What kind of crooked, awkward, narrow, humped, deformed argumentation is this! Indeed, even now I hear the education of our day, and my ears are again ringing with clear, historical 'self-evidences,' with clear, precocious, pitiless, historical rationalizings! Mark this, you unprofaned Nature: you have become old and for thousands of years this starry heaven has rested over you – but you have never yet heard such an educated [gebildetes] and, at bottom, wicked chatter [Gerede] as this present time loves ! Thus you are proud, my good Teutons, of your poets and artists? You point to them with your fingers, and you plume yourself with them in the face of foreign countries? And because it has cost you no trouble to have them among you, thus make therefrom a most sweet theory that you also need not give yourselves any trouble about them in the future? Is that not true, my inexperienced children, they come by themselves, the stork brings them to you! Who would be able to speak of midwives! Now, my good ones, to you a serious instruction belongs: What? You are permitted to be proud on this ground, that all of the named gleaming and noble spirits have been prematurely suffocated, consumed, extinguished through you, through your barbarism?[18] How are you able to think without shame on Lessing, who perished by your stupidity [Stumpfheit], in a struggle with your laughable blockheads and idols [Klötzen und Götzen],[19] under the abuse of your theater, your scholars, your theologians, without being permitted one single time to risk that eternal flight for which he had come into the world? And what do you feel at Winckelmann's memory, who, in order to free his view from your grotesque foolishness, went begging for help to the Jesuits, whose disgraceful conversion falls back on you and will cling to you as an

18   This passage, starting here, was later published almost verbatim in section four of the untimely meditation on David Strauss, *KSA* 1.183.14.

19   This is likely an allusion to Lessing's polemics against C. A. Klötz and J. M. Goeze. See *Antiquarische Briefe* (which argue with Klötz about art) and *Eine Parabel. Nebst einer kleinen Bitte und einem eventualen Absagungsschreiben an den Herrn Pastor Goeze in Hamburg* and *Anti-Goeze. D. i.Notgedrungener Beitrage zu den "Freiwilligen Beitragen" des Hrn. Past. Goeze* (which argue with Goeze about theology).

indelible blot? You are even able to name Schiller's name and do not blush? Look at his picture! The blazing, sparkling eye that despisingly flies right over you, this deathly reddened cheek – that says nothing to you? There you had such a masterful and divine plaything, that was smashed by you. And, still further, take away Goethe's friendship out of this heavy-hearted, hurried life, coursing toward death – then it would lie on you to make it extinguish still faster. You have helped with respect to none of our great geniuses – and now you want to make of it a dogma that no more will be helped? Rather for every one you were, up till this moment, the 'resistance of the stupid [stumpfen] world,' which Goethe names by name in his epilogue to *The Bell*,[20] for every one you were the annoying stupid ones or the envious narrow-minded ones or the wicked selfish ones. Despite you those ones created their works, against you they turned their attacks, and thanks to you they died too early, their workday incomplete, broken, or deadened under battles.[21] Who can imagine what these heroic men had been allotted to achieve, if that true German spirit had spread out its protecting roof over them in a powerful institution, that spirit that, without such an institution, drags its existence along, isolated, crumbled, degenerated. All those men were condemned to death: and it belongs to a belief become mad, a belief in the rationality of everything that happens, in order with it to excuse your guilt. And not those men alone! The accusers step out against you from all the regions of intellectual distinction: whether I look at all the poetic or philosophic or painting or plastic gifts and not only at the gifts of the highest degree, all over I observe those not-yet-become-ripe, those overexcited or those too early exhausted, those singed or frozen before they blossomed, all over I smell that 'resistance of the stupid world,' i.e., *your* guiltiness. That is what I mean to say when I demand educational institutions and find the condition of those that so name themselves worthy of pity. Whoever pleases to call this an 'ideal demand' and generally 'ideal' and probably

20 Goethe's *Epilogue to Schiller's "The Bell"*, line 52.
21 Here ends the passage repeated in *David Strauss*, KSA 1.184.5.

indeed therewith means to pay me off with praise, for them the answer serves that the present one is simply a vulgarity and a disgrace, and that whoever demands warmth in lean frost must become wild if one calls this an 'ideal demand.' Here the question is about clear, pressing, evident realities: whoever feels something of it, he knows that it is here a necessity like frost and hunger. But whoever feels nothing of it – now, he has then at least a measuring stick in order to measure where what I call 'education' ceases and at which of the pyramid's freestones the spheres divided themselves, the one ruled from beneath and the other, the one ruled from above."

The philosopher appeared to have become very heated: we exhorted him to walk around somewhat again, whereas he had spoken his last speech standing in the neighborhood of that tree stump that served as the target butt for our pistol arts. It became wholly silent among us for a time. Slowly and reflectively we strode up and down. We felt much less shame to have brought forth such foolish arguments than a certain restitution of our personality: precisely after the heated and, for us, unflattering address we believed ourselves closer to the philosopher, indeed we felt situated more personally.

For so miserable is the human being that he comes near to a stranger so quickly through nothing so much as when the latter lets a weakness, a defect be noticed. That our philosopher became heated and used abusive words bridged over somewhat the up-till-then solely felt, shy deference: for one, who finds such an observation scandalous, let it be added that this bridge oftentimes leads from the most distant reverence to personal love and to sympathy. And this sympathy strode forth, after that feeling of the restitution of our personality, gradually ever stronger. For what were we leading the old man around here at nighttime between tree and rock? And since he had given in to us on this, why did we not find a calmer and more modest form for us to be instructed; why must we three express our opposition in such an awkward way?

For now we already noticed how unconsidered, unprepared, and inexperienced our objections were, how much precisely in them resounded the echo of *the* present, whose voice the old one now for once did not want to hear on the subject of education. Moreover, our objections had not actually sprung forth purely from the intellect: the reason, which was excited and provoked to opposition through the speeches of the philosopher, appeared to lie somewhere else. Perhaps merely the instinctive anxiety spoke out of us as to whether precisely our own persons [Individuen] would be considered advantageously by such views as those the philosopher had. Perhaps all those earlier illusions [Einbildungen], which we had made about our own education, now in necessity press together to find at any price reasons against a kind of consideration through which of course our pretended claim to education would be properly, thoroughly rejected. But with opponents, who feel so personally the weight of an argument, one should not contend; or as the moral for our case would run: such opponents should not contend, should not contradict.

Thus we walked next to the philosopher ashamed, sympathetic, dissatisfied with ourselves and convinced more than ever that the gray old man must be in the right and that we had done him an injustice. How far behind now lay that youthful dream of our educational institution, how clearly we recognized the danger which we had slipped past up till now only by accident, namely to sell ourselves completely[22] to the educational system, which has spoken to us alluringly from those boyhood years up to our Gymnasium time. Wherein did it lie indeed, that we did not still stand in the public chorus of its admirers? Perhaps only therein, that we were still real students, that we ourselves could still withdraw, out of the greedy grasping and pressing, out of the restless and rushing dashing of the waves of public opinion, to that island soon now also to be washed away!

Overcome by such thoughts we were in mind[23] to address the philosopher, as he suddenly turned toward us and began with a milder voice: "I should not wonder when you conduct yourselves

22 More literally, "with skin and hair."
23 More literally, "in concept."

youthfully, imprudently, and hastily. For you have hardly reflected yet at any time seriously about that which you hear from me. Let yourself take time, carry it around with you, but think thereupon day and night. For now you are placed on the crossroad, now you know where both ways lead. Traveling upon the one you will be welcomed by your time, it will not be lacking in garlands and other signs of victory for you: monstrous parties will support you, behind your back will stand just as many like-minded ones as in front of you. And when the first man pronounces a battle cry thus it is repeated in all the ranks. Here the first duty is to fight in rank and file; the second: to annihilate all those who do not want to be put in rank and file. The other way brings you together with rarer travel companions; it is more difficult, more winding [verschlungener], and steeper: those that walk upon the first path mock you, because you step there more laboriously, they probably even attempt to lure you over to them. But when some time both paths should cross, so you will be mistreated, pushed to the side, or they shy away from you and isolate you.

"Now what would an educational institution signify to the different kinds of travelers of the two ways? That monstrous swarm that presses toward its goals upon the first path, understand thereby an institution through which it is itself organized into rank and file and from which everything that possibly strives after higher and more remote goals is separated and detached. To be sure they understand how to bring resplendent words for their tendencies into circulation: they speak, e.g., of the 'development on all sides of free personality within fixed, common, national and humane-moral [menschlich-sittlicher] convictions,' or name as their goal 'the foundation of a tranquil people's state upon reason, culture, and justice.'

"For the other smaller troop an educational institution is something thoroughly different. In the protection of a fixed organization, they want to prevent the chance that they themselves would be washed away and driven apart from each other by that swarm, that their individuals would lose sight of their noble and elevated task in premature fatigue or be diverted, degenerated, destroyed.

These individuals should complete their work, that is the meaning [Sinn] of their communal institution – and indeed a work, that, as it were, should be purified from the imprint [Spur] of the subject and carried out above the interplay of the times, as the clear mirroring of the eternal and unchanging essence of the thing. And all who have a part in that institution should take trouble through such a purification of subjectivity to prepare the birth of the genius and the begetting of his work. Not a few, even from the ranks of those with second- and third-class gifts are predestined [bestimmt] for such service [Mithelfen] and only come to the feeling of living up to their duty in the service [Dienste] of such a true educational institution. But now precisely these gifts are diverted from their course, and their instincts are alienated by the incessant seductions[24] of that fashionable 'culture' [Kultur]. This seduction[25] addresses itself to their egoistic emotions, to their weaknesses and vanities. Precisely that spirit of the times whispers to them, 'Follow me! There you are servants [Diener], helpers [Gehülfen], tools, outshined by higher natures, your peculiar character never joyful, drawn up in ropes, laid in chains, as slaves, yes, as automatons: here, with me, you enjoy as masters your free personality, your gifts may shine for yourself, with them you yourself will stand in the first position, a monstrous following will attend you, and the acclamation of public opinion will please you more than a nobly administered commendation from the height of the genius.' The best ones of all are now overcome by such allurements, and at bottom the degree of the gift probably hardly matters here, or whether one is open to those kind of voices or not, rather the height and degree of a certain moral [sittlichen] elevation, the instinct toward heroism, toward sacrifice – and finally a secure need of culture, become a habit [Sitte], introduced by a proper education [Erziehung]: as

24 I translate "Verführungskünste" as "seductions" here, but it is more literally "seductive arts" and is translated thus later.

25 Here the German is "Versuchung." The difference between Verführung and Versuchung is that between misleading or misdirecting others and pursuing an improper seeking oneself.

that which is, as I already said, before everything obedience and habituation [Gewöhnung] to the discipline of the genius. But precisely of such a discipline, of such habituation [Gewöhnung], the institutions that one now calls 'educational institutions' know as little as nothing: although I have no doubt that the Gymnasium was meant originally as one of those true educational institutions, or at least as a preparatory arrangement, and in the wonderful, deeply thoughtful, excited times of the Reformation the first bold steps of such a course were really taken, likewise that in the time of our Schiller, our Goethe, again something of that disgracefully suppressed [abgeleiteten] or made secret need was noticed, almost like a germ of that wing of which Plato speaks in the *Phaedrus*[26] and which gives wings to the soul and carries it up at any contact with the beautiful – toward the realm of the unchangeable, purely formed archetypes [Urbilder] of things."

– "Oh, my revered and distinguished teacher," the companion now began, "After you have cited the divine Plato and the world of Ideas, I no longer believe that you are angry with me, as much as I also have deserved your disapproval and your anger through my previous speech. As soon as you speak, that Platonic wing stirs itself in me; and only in intervals do I, as chariot driver of my soul, have real trouble with the resisting, wild, and unruly horse that Plato has also described and of which he says it is crooked and hulking, with a stiff nape, a short neck and flat nose, colored black, gray eyes, blood-shot, in the ears shaggy and hard of hearing, ready at all times for sacrilege and crime and hardly tractable through whip and spur. Think then, thereupon, how long I have lived at a distance from you and how precisely even on me all those seductive arts [Verführungskünste], of which you spoke, were able to try themselves, perhaps, indeed, not without some success even if almost unnoticed by me myself. I grasp precisely now, more strongly than ever, how necessary an institution is that merely makes it possible to live together with the rare men of true culture in order to have in them leaders and guiding stars. How strongly I feel the

26   *Phaedrus* 253 d – e.

danger of solitary traveling! And when I, as I said to you, fancied saving myself by flight from the bustle and direct contact with the spirit of the time, so was this flight itself a deception. Continuously, from countless veins, with every breath that atmosphere flows into us, and no solitude is solitary and distant enough that it does not know how to reach us with its fog and clouds. Disguised as doubt, as profit, as hope, as virtue, the images [Bilder] of that culture sneak around us in the most exchangeable costumery: and even here in your proximity, i.e., almost in the hand of a true hermit of culture that jugglery knows how to seduce us. How constantly and loyally must that small troop of a culture that could almost be called sectarian, be wakeful among themselves! How they must reciprocally strengthen themselves! How rigorously must the misstep be reprimanded, how sympathetically it is forgiven! So now forgive me too, my teacher, after you have rebuked me so seriously!"

"You use a language, my good one," said the philosopher, "that I do not like and which reminds of a religious conventicle.[27] I have nothing to do therewith. But your Platonic horse pleased me, for its sake you too should be forgiven. I exchange my nursing animal for this horse. Besides I have little desire left to walk around still further with you here in the cool air. My friend, whom I was awaiting, is indeed crazy enough probably even still to come up here at midnight when once he has promised it. But I wait in vain upon the sign agreed upon between us: it remains incomprehensible to me what has detained him up till now. For he is punctual and exact as we old ones are accustomed to be and which the youths today hold to be old-fashioned.[28] This time he has left me in the lurch: it is vexatious! Now just follow me! It is time to go!"

– In this moment something new showed itself. –

27 A conventicle is a secret meeting for unsanctioned or irregular religious worship.
28 More literally, "old fatherish."

LECTURE V

My honored listeners!

If that which I have told you of the various excited speeches of our philosopher, conducted in nocturnal silence, was received by you with some sympathy, thus the last reported ill-humored resolution of the same must have struck you in a similar way as it, at that time, struck us. Namely, he suddenly announced to us that he wanted to go: left in the lurch by his friend and little quickened by what we, together with his companion, knew how to offer in such a wilderness, he appeared now to want to break off hastily the useless, prolonged stay on the mountain. The day likely counted as lost to him; and, as it were, shaking it off of himself he certainly would have liked to be able to cast the memory of our acquaintance behind him. And so he drove us, unwilling, to begin to go, when a new phenomenon compelled him to stand still and the already raised foot again sank hesitatingly.

A colored gleam of light and a crackling, fast-dying noise from the region of the Rhine captivated our attention and directly thereupon a slow melodic phrase, in harmony with, indeed strengthened by, numerous youthful voices, stretched out from the distance over to us. "This is indeed his signal," called the philosopher, "My friend yet comes, and I have not waited in vain. It will be a midnight reunion – how can we indeed inform him that now I am still here? Up! Your pistols [Pistolenschützen], now show your artistry [Künste] for once! Do you hear the severe rhythm of that melody greeting us? Mark this rhythm and repeat it in the sequence of your explosions!"

This was a task after our taste and our capacity; we loaded as quickly as possible, and, after briefly coming to an understanding, we raised our pistols toward star-illuminated heights, while that insistent melody [Tonfolg] in the depths, after a brief repetition, died away. The first, the second, and the third shots went out smartly into the night – then the philosopher shouted, "False beat!" For suddenly we had become untrue to our rhythmic task. Immediately after the third shot, a shooting star came and flew down as swift as an arrow, and almost involuntarily the fourth and fifth shots sounded at the same time, in the direction of its descent.

"False beat!" shouted the philosopher, "Who told you to aim toward the shooting star! It collapses already by itself, without you; one must know what one wants when one handles weapons."

In this moment, carried over from the Rhine, that melody repeated itself, now intoned by numerous and clear voices. "They have yet understood us," my friend called laughing, "And who can even resist when such a luminous apparition comes precisely within shooting distance?" –

"Silence!" the companion interrupted him, "What kind of swarm can it be that sings this signal toward us? I should guess about twenty to forty voices, powerful, manly voices – and whence does that swarm greet us? It appears still not to have left the opposite bank of the Rhine – yet we must indeed be able to look for it from our bank. Come thither quickly!"

In that place, namely, upon which we had up till now been walking up and down, in the proximity of that enormous tree stump, the view toward the Rhine was cut into sections by the dense, dark, and tall woods. On the other hand, I have already said that from out of that calm place, somewhat lower than the level plain on the heights of the mountain, one had a view through the treetops, and that precisely the Rhine, with the island Nonnenwörth in its arms, filled out for the observer the middle point of the rounded cut-out. We ran hastily, yet with care for the old grey philosopher, toward this calm place: it was pitch black in the forest, and guiding the philosopher on the right and on the left, we guessed the beaten way more than we perceived it.

We had hardly reached the bank when a fiery, dull, broad, and restless light, clearly from the other side of the Rhine, fell into our eyes. "Those are torches," I called. "Nothing is more certain than that my comrades from Bonn are over there and that your friend must be in their midst. These ones have sung; these ones will give him an escort. Look! Listen! Now they are climbing into little boats: in a little more than a half-hour the torchlight procession will have arrived over here."

The philosopher sprang back. "What did you say?" he replied, "Your comrades from Bonn, thus students, my friend came with students?" –

This almost wrathfully advanced question stirred us up. "What do you have against students?" we retorted and received no answer. Only after a while the philosopher began slowly, in a plaintive tone and almost addressing one still distant: "Thus even at midnight, my friend, even upon the lonely mountain we will not be alone, and you yourself bring a troop of student disturbers of the peace up here to me. Yet you know that I get out of the way of this *genus omne*[1] gladly and warily. I do not understand you in this, my distant friend: it must indeed say something when we find ourselves together in a reunion after a long separation and pick out for it such a remote corner and such an unusual hour. Why should we want a chorus of witnesses, and of such witnesses! Indeed what calls us together for today is least of all a sentimental, softhearted need: for we have both learned with time how to be able to live alone and in dignified isolation. Not for our own sake, for instance in order to cultivate tender feelings or in order pathetically to present a scene of friendship, have we decided to see each other here; rather here, where I once came across you in a memorable hour, solemnly isolated, we wanted to tend [pflegen][2] the most serious counsel with one another almost as knights of a new Vehmic court.[3] Let those who understand us listen closely, but why do you

1   A shortened version of *hoc genus omne*, "all this sort." Horace, *Satires*, Book II.6.

2   Pflegen is translated elsewhere as "cultivate."

3   A Vehmic (or Fehmic) court was a tribunal of unknown origin but traceable back in time to the age of Charlemagne. The court was held, often in secret, often in the open air on grassy hills, and its proceedings were run by an elaborately ordered secret society, the Holy Order of the Vehm. The term "Vehm" may have been derived from an Arabic word for wisdom. Vehmic courts had a powerful and,

bring along a swarm who certainly do not understand us! I do not recognize you in this, my distant friend!"

We did not consider it proper to interrupt such an ill-humored [ungemuth] lamenter: and he grew dumb in melancholy, yet we did not dare to say to him how much this mistrusting rejection of students must have vexed us.

Finally the companion turned to the philosopher and said: "You remind me, my teacher, of the fact that you also indeed in an earlier time, before I was acquainted with you, have lived in several universities and that rumors from that period about your dealings with students, about the method of you instruction, are still in circulation. From the tone of resignation with which you have just spoken of the students, many may suspect[4] peculiar, irritating experiences; but I believe much more that you have experienced and seen just that, which everyone experiences and sees there, but that you have judged this more strongly and more correctly than any other. For so much have I learned from your company, that the most noteworthy, most instructive, and decisive experiences and events are the everyday ones. However, precisely that which lies before all eyes as a monstrous riddle is understood by the fewest as a riddle, and that for the few genuine[5] philosophers just these problems remain lying untouched in the middle of the street and, as it were, under the feet of the multitude, in order then to be carefully raised up by them and from then on to shine as precious stones[6] of knowledge. Perhaps say to us, in the brief pause that remains to us still until the arrival of your friend, something about your knowledge and experiences in the sphere of the

according to legend, sinister jurisdiction, especially in Westphalia. The only punishment meted out by the court was death, and the executions were performed without delay. Vehmic courts were officially abolished by order of Julian Bonaparte, king of Westphalia, in 1811.

4   Or "guess."

5   Rechten could also be translated as "proper" or, more literally, "right."

6   More literally, "noble stones."

university and therewith complete the circle of considerations to which we have been involuntarily urged with respect to our educational institutions. Moreover, permit us to remind you that you, at an earlier stage of your discussion, even made me a promise of that kind.[7] Starting from the Gymnasium, you claimed for it an extraordinary significance: to its educational goal, according to how it is put, all other institutions must measure themselves, in errors in its tendency everyone has to suffer along. Such a significance, as a motive center, now the universities themselves can no longer lay claim to, which with their present formation, at least according to an important camp, may be held only as extensions of the tendency of the Gymnasiums. Here you promised me later a detailed statement: something that perhaps even our student friends could testify to, who possibly have listened in to our conversation at that time."

"To this we testify," I replied. The philosopher turned himself toward us and replied: "Now, if you have really eavesdropped, thus you can at once describe what you, after everything that was said, understood by the present tendency of the Gymnasiums. Moreover, you stand still near enough to this sphere to be able to measure my thoughts by your experiences and feelings."

My friend answered, quickly and adroitly, as is his manner, approximately the following: "Up till now we had always believed that the single purpose of the Gymnasium was to prepare for the university. But this preparation should make us independent enough for the extraordinarily free position of a university man [Akademiker]. For it seems to me that in no area of the present day life is so much left to be decided and to be used[8] by the individual, as in the realm of student life. He must be able to lead himself out upon a broad plain for several years completely freely given over to him: thus the Gymnasium will have to attempt to make him independent."

I continued the speech of my comrade. "It seems to me even," I said, "that everything that you, certainly with justice, have to blame in the Gymnasium, is only the necessary means, in order to beget for

7   See the second lecture, p. 44 (footnote 5).
8   Or "disposed of."

such a youthful age a kind of independence or at least the belief there-in. The German instruction should serve this independence: the indi-vidual must early become happy about his views and intentions [Ansichten und Absichten] in order to be able to walk alone without crutches. Therefore he will be encouraged already early toward pro-duction and still earlier toward sharp judgment and criticism. Even if the Latin and Greek studies are not in a position to set a student aflame for distant antiquity, yet with the method with which they are pursued the scientific sense is probably thus awakened, the desire for a more rigorous causality of knowledge, the appetite for finding and inventing [Finden und Erfinden]: how many may become lastingly seduced to the enticements of science by a new kind of reading, found in the Gymnasium, snatched up with youthful groping! Many kinds of things must the Gymnasium student learn and collect in himself: thereby a drive is probably gradually[9] begotten; escorted by it he then learns and collects at the university independently in a similar way. In short, we believe, it should be the tendency of the Gymnasium to pre-pare and accustom the student so that he afterwards lives and learns further as independently as he must live and learn under the compul-sion of the order of the Gymnasium."

The philosopher laughed at this, yet not precisely good-naturedly, and replied, "There you have given me immediately a beautiful spec-imen of this independence. And precisely it is this independence that so terrifies me and makes me ever so unpleasant [unerquicklich] in the proximity of students of the present. Yes, my good ones, you are ready, you are grown up, nature has broken your mold [Form], and your teachers must gloat over you. What freedom, determination, unconcernedness of judgment, what newness and freshness of insight! You sit in judgment – and all the cultures [Kulturen] of all times run away from it. The scientific sense is inflamed and bursts like a flame out of you – let everyone take care not to be burned by you! If I still include likewise your professors so I receive this same independence yet once again in a more powerful and more charming gradation; never was a time so rich in the most beautiful independence, never has one

9   Or "leisurely."

hated so strongly any slavery, also, of course, the slavery of education [Erziehung] and of culture [Bildung].

"But allow me to measure, for once, this, our independence by the measuring stick of just this culture [Bildung] and to draw into consideration our university only as an educational institution [Bildungsanstalt]. If a foreigner wants to become familiar with our university system, thus he first asks with emphasis: how is the student connected with the university with you? We answer: through the ear, as listener. – The foreigner is astounded. 'Only through the ear?' he asks again. 'Only through the ear,' we answer again. The student listens. When he speaks, when he sees, when he walks, when he is sociable, when he practices the arts, in short, when he lives, he is independent,[10] i.e., not dependent[11] on the educational institution. Very frequently the student immediately writes something as he hears it. These are the moments in which he hangs on the umbilical cord of the university. He can choose what he wants to hear, he does not need to believe what he hears, he can close his ears if he does not like to hear. This is the 'acroamatic'[12] method of teaching.

"But the teacher speaks to these listening students. What he otherwise thinks and does is separated from the perception of the students by a monstrous gap. Frequently the professor reads while he speaks. In general he wants to have as many such listeners as possible, in need he contents himself with a few, almost never with one. One speaking mouth and very many ears with half as many writing hands – that is the external academic apparatus, that is the educational machine of the university in action. Besides, the owner of this mouth is separated from the possessors of the many ears and independent; and they praise this double independence with high glee as 'academic freedom.' Besides, the one can – in order to increase this freedom still further – roughly speak what he wants, the other roughly hear

10   Selbständig means more literally, "self-standing."
11   Unabhängig is often translated as "independent." More literally, it means "not hanging from."
12   From the Greek ἀκροαματικός, meaning "something for hearing only." Acroamatic is a term associated with esoteric oral traditions.

what he wants: only that behind both groups at a discreet distance stands the state, with a certain taut overseer's mien, in order to remind from time to time that it is the purpose, the goal, the be-all-and-end-all of this strange speaking-and-listening procedure.

"We, to whom it must be allowed to consider this surprising phenomenon only as an educational institution, report thus to the inquiring foreigner, that that which is education at our universities goes from the mouth to the ear, that all education [Erziehung] toward culture [Bildung], as was said, is only 'acroamatic.' But since even the listening and the selection of what is listened to is left to the independent decision of the academic, liberal student, since he, on the other hand, can deny credibility and authority[13] to everything listened to, thus in a rigorous sense all education [Erziehung] toward culture [Bildung] falls to him himself, and the independence striven toward by the Gymnasium now points to itself with the highest pride as 'academic self-education [Selbsterziehung] toward culture [Bildung]' and parades its most radiant plumage.

"A happy time, in which the youths are wise and cultured [gebildet] enough, in order to be able to keep themselves in leading strings! Unsurpassable Gymnasiums that succeed in cultivating [pflanzen] independence where other times thought dependence, discipline, subordination, obedience must be cultivated and all conceit of independence must be repulsed! Is it becoming clear to you here, my good ones, why I, on the side of education, prefer[14] to consider the present-day university as an extension of the tendency of the Gymnasium? The education appealed to by the Gymnasium strides, as something whole and ready, with picky demands into the gates of the university: *it* demands, it gives laws, it sits in judgment. Do not deceive yourselves so about the cultured [gebildeten] students: this one is, as far as he even believes himself to have received the holy orders of culture [Bildungsweihen], always still the Gymnasium student formed by the hands of his teacher: as one now, since his academic isolation, and after he has left the Gymnasium, who therewith

13   Reading, with Schlechta, Autorität for Auktorität.
14   More literally, love.

} 107 {

is deprived wholly of all further formation and guidance toward culture [Bildung], in order from now on to live by himself and to be free.

"Free! Test this freedom you knowers of human beings! Built up upon the hollow[15] ground of the present-day Gymnasium culture [Gymasialkultur], upon a crumbling foundation, its structure stands badly made[16] and unsafe with the blowing of the whirlwind. Look at the free student, the herald of educational independence, divine him [17] in his instincts, construe him from his needs! How does his education strike you when you know to measure this by three barometers [Gradmessern]: once by his need for philosophy, then by his instinct for art, and finally by Greek and Roman antiquity as the embodied categorical imperative of all culture [Kultur].

"The human being is so surrounded by the most serious and most difficult problems that, led to them in the right way, in time he comes to that lasting, philosophic wonder,[18] upon which alone, as upon a fruitful subsoil, can grow a deep and noble culture. Most frequently probably his own experiences lead him to these problems, and especially in the stormy period of youth, almost every personal event mirrors in a doubled glimmer, as an exemplification of an everyday matter and at the same time as an eternal, astonishing [erstaunlichen] problem, worthy of explanation. At this age in which his experiences almost look ringed about with metaphysical rainbows the human being is in need in the highest degree of a guiding hand, because he suddenly and almost instinctively has convinced himself of the ambiguity of existence and has lost the firm soil of the previously entertained, received opinions.

"This natural condition of the highest neediness must be held, logically, as the worst enemy of that beloved independence, to which the educated [gebildete] youth of the present should be drawn. To suppress and cripple it, to divert or to starve it, to that end all those youths of 'modern times,' already resting in the lap of the 'self-evident,'

15   Or "clay," or "earthen."
16   Or "set slanting."
17   Or "guess him".
18   Erstaunen is more literally "astonishment."

eagerly exert themselves: and the favorite means is to paralyze that natural philosophic drive through the so-called 'historical culture.' One still young system, standing in scandalous world-wide fame, has discovered the formula for this self-annihilation of philosophy: and now it shows itself ready generally, with the historical consideration of things, such a naïve unreflectiveness, to bring the most irrational thing to 'reason' and to allow the blackest thing to be held as white, that one would like to ask more frequently, with a parodic application of that Hegelian principle: 'Is this irrationality real?' Ah, precisely this irrationality now alone appears 'real,' i.e., to be active, and to be disposed to think[19] this kind of reality fit for explanation by history counts as authentic 'historical culture' [Bildung]. The philosophic drive of our youths has metamorphosized [verpuppt][20] into this: the peculiar philosophies of the universities today appear to have conspired to strengthen the young academics in this.

"Thus slowly has strode into the place of a deeply thoughtful interpretation of the eternally same problems a historical, yes even a philological, weighing out and questioning: what this or that philosopher has thought or not, whether this or that writing can justly be ascribed to him, or whether this or that kind of reading deserves priority. To such a neutral dealing with philosophy, our students in the philosophical seminaries are now incited: wherefore I have long been accustomed to consider such a science as a branching-off of philology and to esteem its advocates accordingly, whether they are good philologists or not. Therefore now, of course, *philosophy itself* is banished from the university: with which our first question concerning the educational value of the universities is answered.

"How this same university behaves toward *art* is not at all to be admitted without shame: it does not behave at all. Of artistic thinking, learning, striving, comparing is here not once one indication to be found, and quite no one would be able to speak in earnest of a vote by the university for the advancement of the most important national art

19 More literally, "ready to hold".
20 Perhaps this would be most literally rendered as "pupated." The Greek-based Metamorphose is translated later as "metamorphosis."

projects. Whether a single teacher feels himself accidentally, personally assigned to art or whether a chair for an aestheticizing literary historian is founded, herewith comes not at all into the consideration: rather that the university as a whole is not in a position to hold the academic youth in a rigorous artistic discipline and that here it wholly willlessly lets happen, whatever happens, therein lies an oh-so-cutting critique of its arrogant claim to want to represent the highest educational institution.

"Up to this point, our academic 'independents' live without philosophy, without art: what kind of need can they have thereafter to grapple with the Greeks and Romans, an inclination toward whom no one any longer has a reason to feign and which, besides, are enthroned in a solitude very difficult to access and in a majestic alienation. The universities of our present day therefore also consequently show no regard at all for such dead educational inclinations [Bildungsneigungen] and found their philological professorships for the training [Erziehung] of new, exclusive generations of philologists, who then attend to the philological preparation of the Gymnasium students: a cycle[21] of life that comes to good for neither the philologists nor the Gymnasium students, that, before everything, chastises the university for the third time for not being that for which it would like pompously to pose as – an educational institution. For take away only the Greeks, together with philosophy and art: on what ladder do you still wish to ascend toward education? For with the attempt to climb the ladder without that help, your erudition[22] – this you must surely allow yourselves to be told – would much more sit on your neck as a heavy burden than it would lend you wings and draw you up.

"If you now, you honest ones, have honestly remained on these three steps of insight and have recognized the present-day student as unfit and unprepared for philosophy, as lacking an instinct for true art, and, in the face of the Greeks, as barbarians imagining themselves to be free, thus you will indeed not flee from him offended, even if you perhaps would rather prevent contacts that are too close. For thus as

21   More literally, "circular course."
22   Or "scholarship."

he is, *he is not guilty*: thus as you have recognized him, he silently, yet horribly accuses the guilty ones.

"You must understand the secret language that this guilty innocent [veschuldet Unschuldige] uses before himself: then you would also learn to understand the inner essence of that independence that likes to be worn externally for show. None of the noble, well-equipped youths remained distant from that restless, tiresome, confounding, enervating educational necessity: for that time, in which he is apparently the single free man in a clerks' and servants' reality, he pays for that grandiose illusion of freedom through ever-renewing torments and doubts. He feels that he cannot lead himself, he cannot help himself: then he dives poor in hopes into the daily world and into daily work: the *most trivial* activity envelops him, his members sink into flabbiness. Suddenly he again rouses himself: he still feels the power, not waned, that enabled him to hold himself aloft. Pride and noble resolution form [bilden] and grow in him. It terrifies him to sink so early into the narrow, petty moderation of a specialty,[23] and now he grasps after supports and pillars in order not to be dragged along in that course. In vain! These supports give way; for he had made a mistake and held tight to brittle reeds. In an empty and disconsolate mood he sees his plans go up in smoke: his condition is abominable and undignified: he alternates between overexcited activity and melancholic enervation. Then he is tired, lazy, fearful of work, terrified in the face of everything great, and hating himself. He dissects [zergliedert][24] his capacities and thinks he is looking into a hollow or chaotically filled space. Then again he plunges from the heights of the dreamed of self-knowledge into an ironic skepticism. He strips his struggle of its importance and feels himself ready for any real, albeit low use [Nützlichkeit]. He now seeks his consolation in hasty, incessant action in order to hide from himself under it. And thus his helplessness and the lack of a leader toward culture [Bildung] drives him from one form of existence into another: doubt, upswing, life's necessity, hope, despair, everything throws him to and fro, as a sign, that all the stars

23   More literally, "specialization."
24   More literally, "dismembers."

above him according to which he could pilot his ship are extinguished.

"That is the image of that famed independence, that academic freedom, reflected in the souls that are best and truly in need of education: over against which these rough and reckless natures that enjoy their freedom in the barbaric sense do not come into consideration. For these show, in their low-natured [gearteten] pleasure and in their workmanlike early narrowness[25] that for them precisely this element is right: against which there is nothing to say at all. But their pleasure truly does not make up for the suffering of a single youth, driven toward culture [Kultur] and in need of a leader, who, in annoyance, finally lets fall the reins and begins to despise himself. This is the guiltless innocent [schuldlos Unschuldige]: for who has burdened him with the unendurable burden of standing alone? Who has incited him to independence at an age in which devotion to a great leader and an enthusiastic following on the track of the master are, as it were, usually the natural and most urgent[26] needs.

"There is something uncanny in reflecting on the effects to which the violent suppression of such noble needs must lead. Whoever, in proximity and with a penetrating eye, reviews the most dangerous promoters and friends of that pseudo-culture [Pseudokultur] of the present, so hated by me, finds only too frequently among them such degenerated[27] and derailed human beings of culture driven by an inner desperation into a hostile rage against culture [Kultur], to which no one would show them the entrance. It is not the worst and meanest that we then find again as journalists and newspaper writers in the metamorphosis of despair; yes, the spirit of a certain now-very-cultivated species of literature should directly be characterized as desperate studentdom. How else should, e.g., that once-well-known 'Young Germany'[28] with its up-to-this-moment, rankly proliferating epigones be understood! Here we discover a need for culture [Bildungsbedürfniß]

25   Or "limitedness."

26   Nächsten means "nearest" or, more literally, "most next."

27   Entartete means literally "moved away from type" and is related to "gearteten," translated as "natured" above.

28   Junges Deutschland , "Young Germany," was a term first made wide-

almost become wild, which finally inflames itself up to the shout: I am culture [Bildung]. There before the gates of the Gymnasiums and universities, the culture [Kultur] of these institutions roves about. It has run away from them and is now acting as sovereign; of course without their erudition: so that, e.g., the novel writer Gutzkow should be taken hold of as the best image of the modern, already literary Gymnasium student.

"A degenerated human being of culture [Bildungsmenschen] is a serious thing: it affects us fearsomely to observe that our collected learned and journalistic public carries the signs of this degeneration within itself. How else can one do justice to our learned scholars when they indefatigably look on or even help with the works of the journalistic seduction of the people, how otherwise, if not through the supposition [Annahme] that their erudition may be for them something similar to that which for those others the writing of novels is, namely, a flight from themselves, an ascetic deadening of their drive toward culture [Bildungstriebs], a desperate annihilation of the individual. From our degenerate literary art just as probably as from the insanely swelling production of books by our scholars wells forth the same sigh: Oh, that we could forget ourselves! It does not succeed: memory, not suffocated by whole mountains of heaped-up, printed paper, repeats still from time to time: 'A degenerated human being of culture [Bildungsmenschen]! Born to culture [Bildung] and educated [erzogen] to lack of culture [Unbildung]! Helpless barbarian, slave of the

ly known by Wolfgang Menzel's savage criticism in 1835 of Karl Gutzkow's novel *Wally die Zweiflerin*. The term "Young Germany" was generally taken to indicate a tightly connected and well-organized, perhaps even conspiratorial, movement, but that was likely not the case. Leading figures among the Young Germans included Karl Gutzkow and Heinrich Heine. Young Germany was characteristically identified with a tendency toward the liberal ideas of political reform, religious tolerance, and sexual emancipation. Some Young Germans were more revolutionary in their inclinations and tended to call for action. Young Germany as a whole tended to identify with the July Revolution in France in 1830 and with the European revolutions of 1848.

day, locked in the chains of the moment and hungering – eternally hungering!'

"Oh the miserable guilty-innocents [verschuldet-Unschuldigen]! For they lack something, each of them must have come up against this. They lack a true educational institution that could give them goals, masters, methods, models, fellows and from whose interior the powerful and elevating breath of the true German spirit would stream toward them. Thus they starve in the wilderness; thus they degenerate into enemies of that spirit which at bottom is intimately related to them; thus they pile up guilt upon guilt more heavily than any other generation ever has piled up, soiling the pure, desecrating the holy, pre-canonizing the false and the phony. In them you may come to consciousness about the educational power of our universities and lay before yourselves in all seriousness the question: What do you promote in them? German erudition, German inventiveness, the honorable German drive toward knowledge, Germany industry, capable of sacrifice, beautiful and lordly things for which other nations will envy you, indeed the most beautiful and lordly things in the world, if over all of them that true German spirit lay spread out like a dark cloud, flashing lightning, fructifying, consecrating. But you are afraid in the face of this spirit and hence another filmy mist [Dunstschicht], muggy and heavy, has condensed over your universities, under which your noble youths breath laboriously and oppressively, under which the best ones perish.

"There was in this century a tragically serious and singularly instructive attempt to disperse that filmy mist and to open up the view for the future in the direction of the high cloud-walking [Wolkengange] of the German spirit. The history of the universities contains no other similar attempt, and whoever wants emphatically to demonstrate what is here necessary to do will never be able to find a clearer example. This is the phenomenon of the old original 'Burschenschaft.'[29]

"In the war the youth had carried home the unexpected worthiest prize of battle, the freedom of the fatherland: with this garland he

29   The Burschenschaft was a student movement that grew out of the Wars of Liberation (against Napoleon). The first Burschenshaft was

pompously mused about nobler things. Turning back to the university he felt, breathing hard, that muggy and corrupted breath that lay over the scene of the university education.[30] Suddenly he saw with terrified, wide-open eyes the un-German barbarism, artfully hidden here among eruditions of all kinds, suddenly he discovered his own comrades as they, leaderless, were abandoned to a repulsive youthful giddiness. And he became angry. With the same mien of the proudest indignation he raised himself, with which his Friedrich Schiller once may have recited '*The Robbers*'[31] before companions: and if this one had given his play the image of a lion and the motto 'in tyrannos,'[32] thus was his youth himself that lion, readying for the spring: and really all 'tyrants' trembled. Yes, these indignant youths looked, to the

founded in Jena in 1815, and similar student associations were soon formed at many other universities. Festivals and public declarations of the national unity of all the Burschenshaften followed in the next few years. The Burschenshaft opposed reactionary government policies and strove for a unified Germany. After the assassination of August von Kotzebue by a member of the Burschenshaft, the organization was banned in 1819. As a result of this the Burschenshaft became a secret society and grew more radical. The students went so far as to attack the police headquarters in Frankfurt in 1832. In the second half of the century the nature of the Burschenshaft changed, and it turned into a union of social clubs of nationalistic and anti-Semitic character.

30 There is a reasonably strong parallelism between these lines and the opening few speeches of Karl von Moor in Act I, Scene 2 of *The Robbers*.

31 Schiller's first play. It first appeared in print in 1781. It is a play involving young men who have come back from the Seven Year's War and, unable to reintegrate into society, become a large and dangerous band of highwaymen. The edition to which Nietzsche refers is the "second, improved edition," of 1782, also commonly refered to as the "lion edition." That edition bears the image of a lion rampant above the motto "in tyrannos." Rumor had it that Schiller was responsible for this image, and that with it he was sending a message. Some attribute the phrase "in tyrannos" to the Renaissance humanist Ulrich von Hutten.

32 Latin for "Against the tyrants."

timid and superficial view, not much different from Schiller's robbers: their speeches sounded to anxious eavesdroppers probably as if compared with them Sparta and Rome had been nunneries.[33] The terror concerning these indignant youths was so general that those 'robbers' in the sphere of the court had not once excited its like: of them, indeed, a German prince, according to Goethe's testimony, is once supposed to have expressed the opinion 'If he were God and he had foreseen the emergence of the robbers, thus he would not have created the world.'[34]

"Whence the inconceivable strength of this terror? For those indignant youths were the bravest, most gifted, and purest among their fellows: a magnanimous carelessness, a noble simplicity of habit distinguished them in gesture and dress: the grandest[35] commandment bound them among one another to a rigorous and pious excellence; what could they fear in them? It is never to be brought to clarity how far they deceived by this fear or dissembled or really recognized the justice of it: but a firm instinct spoke out of this fear and out of the disgraceful and senseless persecution. This instinct hated the Burschenschaft twice, with a dogged hatred: first its organization, as the first attempt at a true educational institution and then the spirit of this educational institution, that manly, serious, heavy-hearted, hard, and bold German spirit, that spirit of the miner's son Luther, which has proved sound from the Reformation till now.

"Now think of the *fate* of the Burschenschaft, when I ask: did the German university at that time understand that spirit, as even the German princes, in their hatred, appeared to have understood it? Did they boldly and decisively fling their arms about their noblest sons with the words 'You must kill me, before you kill these'? – I hear your

33 A couple of speeches later in Act I, Scene 2 of *The Robbers*, Karl concludes a speech accepting the leadership of a band of disaffected youths with the promise, "I'll turn Germany into a republic that will make Rome and Sparta look like nunneries."

34 *Conversations with Eckermann*, Wednesday, January 17, 1827. Goethe does not identify the prince in the anecdote.

35 Or "most masterful."

answer: by it you may estimate whether the German university is a German educational institution.

"At that time the student foresaw in what depths a true educational institution must be rooted: namely in an inner renewal and excitation of the purest moral powers. And this should be retold forever of the students to their fame. On the slaughtering field he may have learned what he could learn least of all in the sphere of 'academic freedom': that one needs great leaders, and that all education begins with obedience. And in the midst of the victorious jubilation, thinking of his liberated fatherland he had given himself the promise to remain German. German! Now he learned to understand Tacitus,[36] now he grasped Kant's categorical imperative, now the 'Lyre and Sword' melodies of Karl Maria von Weber[37] charmed him. The gates of philosophy, of art, yes, of antiquity sprang up before him – and in one of the most memorable bloody deeds, in the murder of Kotzebue[38] he revenged, with a deep instinct and enthusiastic short-sightedness, his singular Schiller, too early consumed by the opposition of the stupid world, who could have been a leader, a master, an organizer for him and whom he now missed with such heart-felt rage.

"For that was the doom [Verhängniß] of those portentous students: they did not find the leader that they needed. Gradually they became insecure, disunited, dissatisfied even among one another; unfortunate awkwardnesses betrayed only too soon that there was in all of them a lack of overshadowing genius in their midst: and that

36 Cornelius Tacitus (c. A.D. 56–c. 112/113), Roman historian. Tacitus's presence on this list of things German seems unusual, but it may be due to his *Germania*.

37 Carl Maria Weber (1786–1826), composer and conductor. The "Lyre and Sword" melodies are a patriotic cantata based upon the poems of the war hero Karl Theodor Körner, published posthumously as *Leyer und Schwerdt* (1814). Körner died on the battlefield in the Wars of Liberation.

38 August von Kotzebue (1761 – 1819), popular and prolific author of more than 230 plays. Kotzebue was stabbed to death in his office by a radical member of the Burschenshaft, Karl Ludwig Sand. Cf. *Beyond Good and Evil*, section 244.

mysterious bloody deed betrayed side by side with a terrifying power also the terrifying dangerousness of that lack. They were leaderless – and for that reason they perished.

"For I repeat it, my friends! – all education begins with the opposite of everything that they now prize as academic freedom, with obedience, with subordination, with discipline, with servitude. And as the great leader needs followers [Geführten], so do they need the leader to lead them: here a reciprocal predisposition rules in the order of the spirits, indeed as kind of pre-established harmony.[39] It is this eternal order, toward which, with natural emphasis, things strive again and again, that precisely that culture [Kultur] intends to work against, disturbing and annihilating, that culture [Kultur] that now sits on the throne of the present. It wants to reduce the leaders to the service of *its* pleasure [Frohdienste] or to bring them to the point of dying away [Verschmachten]: it lies in wait for those to be led when they seek after their predestined leaders, and stifles their seeking instinct through intoxicating means. But if despite that those determined for one another find themselves together, struggling and wounded, then there is a deeply excited, delightful feeling, like the resounding of an eternal string music, a feeling that I can only let you guess at through a simile.

"Have you, for once, looked with a little interest at a musical rehearsal at the odd, shriveled, good-natured species of the human race from which the German orchestra is accustomed to form itself? What alternate play by the capricious goddess 'Form'! What noses and

---

39 Pre-established harmony is a doctrine famously associated with Leibniz. Leibniz used this principle to explain the apparent influence that different substances had on each other, for example the soul and body. Leibniz argued that different substances, like soul and body, did not influence each other but were so arranged by the deity from their very beginning that following only the laws of their own divinely formed natures they produced exactly the set of appearances required to give the impression that they were influenced by other substances. Thus body and soul have the appearance of causal relations but in truth only a pre-established harmony. See, e.g., *Postscript of a Letter to Basnage de Beauval*, 1696.

ears, what awkward or shaky-rustling movements! Think for once that you were deaf and had not once dreamed anything of the existence of tones and of music and that you had to enjoy the play of the revolving of the orchestra as plastic artistes: You would, undisturbed by the idealizing effect of the tone, not be able at all to look with satisfaction at the medieval, rough wood-cut manner of this comedy, at this harmless parody of *homo sapiens*.

"Now think in turn of your sense for music returning, your ears opened, and at the head of the orchestra an honorable keeper of the beat [Taktschläger][40] in appropriate activity: the comedy of that configuration is now no longer there for you; you listen – but the spirit of tedium appears to you to go over from the honorable keeper of the beat to his fellows. You see now only sleep, softness, you hear now only the rhythmically inexact, the melodically common and the trivially emoted. The orchestra becomes for you an indifferent, annoying, or downright repulsive mass.

"But finally, with winged imagination, set for once a genius, a real genius in the midst of this mass – immediately you notice something unbelievable. It is as if this genius, in a lightning transmigration of souls, had traveled into all these half-animal bodies and as if now from all of them in turn only *one* demonic eye peered out. But now listen and look – you will never be able to hear enough! When you now consider again the orchestra, loftily storming, or tenderly lamenting, when you sense nimble eagerness[41] in every muscle and rhythmic necessity in every gesture, then you will feel sympathetically what a pre-established harmony between leader and followers is, and how in the order of spirits everything presses toward the construction of an organization of that sort. My simile suggests to you, however, what I probably would understand by a true educational institution and why I, even in the university, do not recognize one such, not in the least."

40   I have perhaps translated this hyper-literally; it could easily be simply translated as "conductor," although Dirigent is perhaps the more ususual term.

41   Or "tension."

APPENDIX A: LETTERS[1]

Letters between Nietzsche and his publisher, Ernst Fritzsch

#204 (3, p. 306) (To Ernst Wilhelm Fritzsch in Leipzig)

Basel 22 March [1872]

Highly esteemed sir,

In this winter, I have held here in Basel, by the commission of the "Academic Society," 6 public lectures on this theme: "On the Future of Our Educational Institutions." Each time I had approximately 300 listeners: from the most diverse sides I have been called upon to get the speeches published. But to me myself it matters very much that they should be well and beautifully published.

When I communicate all this to you thus you will guess the meaning of my letter. Now I know indeed that the theme of these my lectures lies still somewhat more distant from the sphere of your publishing house than "The Birth of Tragedy." In any case I want to make you first of all a proposition: and I would be very pleased, if you should be able to accept it.

---

1 All the letters and selections from letters, with the exception of one from Fritzsch to Nietzsche, included in this appendix, are taken from the *Kritische Studienausgabe.* The letters are identified by both the editors' numeration and by volume and page number. The letter from Fritzsch is from the *Kritische Gesamtausgabe* and is similarly identified. Some of the selections are quite brief, as the rest of the letters from which they were excerpted had little or no obvious connection to *On the Future of Our Educational Institutions.*

My proposition goes along the completely same provisions and the same conditions as with the "Birth." But, for two reasons, the copies must be ready for shipping by May 22. What goes forward in Bayreuth on that day we [both] know: aside from that, on that day the general German Philologists and Teachers Assembly begins in Leipzig. To bring the latter closer to the meaning of the first event and to put into the heart of precisely the teachers the cultural significance of our musical movement is the intention and the quintessence of my lectures.

But, as already hinted at, respected sir – *for* you there is from no side an obligation: if you write me, without reasons: "it is not a go,"[2] then I will understand you completely and consider this letter as settled.

For all that, I permitted myself to turn to no one else *first*, precisely because, with my last book, I had had such an agreeable and estimable experience.

Give me a short note soon and take the letter as it was written: *sincerely*!

Respectfully yours,

Fr. Nietzsche

#301[3] (*KGA* II, II, p. 576) (Ernst Wilhelm Fritzsch to Nietzsche in Basel)

Leipzig, the ¼ 1872

Revered Sir!
My answer to your honoring proposal was delayed somewhat as

2   More literally, "it goes not."
3   This is a letter is to Nietzsche, rather than from Nietzsche. The number assigned to it follows the *Kritische Gesamtausgabe*'s numeration for letters *to* Nietzsche.

a result of the work of the preceding holidays[4] and thus I take the pleasure to myself today first to send off the same.

Of course, will not your new booklet[5] be presumed good in my publishing house; in my opinion the question is rather more this, whether *you* with a closer consideration may see some danger therein? As to what concerns my part, thus you have to have no worry; even the assigned completion date of manufacture I can hold to with a speedy delivery of the manuscript. Thus reflect alone on the drawbacks,[6] which my firm as the place of publication could have for the dissemination of the little work, and have suggestions for the circumnavigation of the same (press advertisement appropriate to the purpose, etc.); thus I ask plainly for advice [Mitteilung]. Now I hope that everything will be done.

With my visit yesterday with the family Reiss in Halle I have seen accidentally with great joy that we are wholly close countrymen: Röcken and Lützen. Is it not remarkable! Mr. Reiss has asked me by the way to greet you heartily from him.

You are coming yet in any case on May 22 to Bayreuth? Or must you visit the Leipzig gathering? From Mr. Wagner I received today a report; when he emigrates with the family to Bayreuth, I have, however, still not been able to learn definitely. You have such inquiries of course more comfortably.

Your next worthy parcel will in no case be allowed to wait long, if your repeated, ripe consideration entails a result other than a negative answer.

This wish at least
Your devoted

E. W. Fritzsch.

4   More literally, "days of celebration."
5   Or "brochure."
6   More literally, "shady sides."

#209 (3, p. 309) (To Ernst Fritzsch, second half of April, 1872)

Highly regarded Sir,

From Lake Geneva you finally receive an answer from me, which I only therefore deliver to you so late, because in the meantime I had to make [treffen][7] a serious and important decision. This touches upon our business insofar as it in any case delays it. My lectures should still be completely reworked and will be cast in another form; wherefore I require above all time. In return you will also receive, when I am ready, a genuine and proper "item for publication," that is, such a one whose effect [Wirksamkeit] should outlast us. Only trust always somewhat in my "literature"; I will never write *much*; but the few I will always offer first to you, presupposing that it has a general character and is not too philologically specialized. . . .

Letters From Nietzsche to Family and Friends

#172 (3, p. 250)

Basel, Sunday 3 December 71

My beloved Mother and Sister,

Heartfelt thanks for the last received letter. I hear with pleasure that things go well for you in Naumburg. However we will not be able to be together for Christmas; I have to hold my 6 lectures "On the Future of Our Educational Institutions" after New Year's and up to now still am hardly able to think about them, my courses at the college busy me so much . . .

---

7   More literally, "meet."

#177 (3, p. 257) (To Erwin Rhode, sometime after December 21, 1871)

. . . I am spending this Christmas alone in Basel and have refused the heartfelt invitations to Tribschen. I require time and solitude in order to reflect on a thing or two about my 6 lectures (Future of Educational Institutions) and to collect myself . . .

#178 (3, p. 260) (To Carl von Gersdorff, Basel, December 23, 1871)

. . . I am anticipating my Christmas celebration in Mannheim and cannot come to Tribschen this time, because I require time and solitude in order to think out my lectures "On the Future of Our Educational Institutions" . . .

#191 (3, p. 277) (To Fransziscka and Elizabeth Nietzsche, January 24, 1872)

. . . then [came] my first lecture on the Future of Educational Institutions with extraordinary results. I speak again next Tuesday, it will probably be overfull. Besides Richard Wagner with his wife is coming over to Basel for this next lecture. . . .

Enclosed I am sending a completely stupid review of my first lecture from the Grenzpost – everything, everything is wrongly understood – that is the amusing thing about it . . . .

#192 (3, pp. 278–80) (To Erwin Rohde in Kiel)

Basel, Sunday [28.] Jan. 72.

My good dear friend,

Recently I have received through Susemihl a preliminary inquiry whether I would accept a professorship in Greifswald, but immediately, for your sake and recommending you, I refused. Is the matter in a farther stage? I have referred to Ribbeck.[8] – Here the matter had indeed become known and awoke a great sympathy for me with the good people of Basel. Although I protested that it was no call, rather only a wholly preliminary inquiry, the studentry had resolved indeed on a torch-lit procession for me, and indeed with the motivation that they want thereby to express how much they esteem and honor my activity up till now in Basel. As for the rest, I declined the torch-lit procession. – Here I am now holding lectures "On the Future of Our Educational Institutions" and have brought it up to a "sensation," here and there to an enthusiasm. Why do we not live near[9] one another! For what all I now carry upon the heart and prepare for the future is in letters not even once to be touched on [berühren]. – I have concluded an alliance with Wagner. You cannot think, as it were, how close we now stand and how our plans meet [sich berühren]. – What I have had to hear about my book is wholly unworthy of belief: wherefore I also write nothing about that – What do you think about that? A monstrous seriousness seizes me with everything that I become aware of about that, because I, in such moods, guess at the future of that, which I had in mind. This life remains very difficult.

In Leipzig bitterness should again rule. No one writes me one little word from there. Not even Ritschl – My good friend, sometime we must again live with one another; it is a holy necessity. I live for some time in a great stream: almost every day brings something astonishing, as also my goals and intentions elevate themselves. – I give you notice, wholly to be kept secret and urging to secrecy, that I among others am preparing a promemoria[10] on the University of Strassburg,[11] as an interpellation at the Reichsrat,[12]

8   Johann Carl Otto Ribbeck (1827–1898), another student of Friedrich Ritschl, author of a number of works, including a biography of Ritschl. Briefly a professor at Basel.
9   Or "with."
10 A memorandum.
11 Nietzsche's spelling of "Stasbourg."
12 The imperial council.

for Bismarck's hands: wherein I want to show, how disgracefully one has neglected a monstrous moment to found a really German educational institution, for the regeneration of the German spirit and for the annihilation of the up till now, so-called[13] "culture" [Cultur]. – Battle with the knife! Or with canons!

> The mounted artillerist, with
> the heaviest gun.

#201 (3, p. 295) (To Erwin Rohde, middle of February 1872)

. . . Here I am fully active thinking on the future of our educational institutions and it will be "organized" and "regenerated" day by day, at any rate for the present only in the head, indeed with a most determined practical "tendency." . . .

#202 (3, p. 296) (To Erwin Rohde)

> Basel, Friday [March 15, 1872]

Finally beloved friend a letter comes from me in return. In the midst of professional obligations and indeed in double such I still had to work out my 6 lectures on the educational institutions [Bildungsschulen]. This will also become my second book,[14] and, let us hope, you will have it in your hands by the middle of the year or earlier. It is hortatory throughout and in comparison with the "Birth" popular or exoteric. I want to have the pleasure myself to address it to the "Philological Union" in Leipzig with a strong introduction. You surely understand this measure in all its facets. . . With the effects achieved here I am extraordinarily satisfied, I have the most serious and most sincere listeners, young men and

13   I am interpreting Nietzsche's abbreviations, "bisher. sog." here.
14   More literally, "writing."

young women and rather the whole student population of the better kind. When I think on my hopes and plans, then you are always present to me, just so that recently once I even became angry and said to myself: "always only Rohde and no one else! The devil take it!" My dear and true comrade, we must even now attempt to fight our way through with one another. If only I also again, with my thoughts on educational institutions, find so unconditionally your interest and endorsement, which was so quickening to me at the baptism of my firstling! It is sad that I can first lay before you all these things published: whereas at bottom between us everything, word for word, ought to be talked through, thought through, lived through. Now there will even come sometime a day where it will be different: I believe in that. . . .

#206 (3, p. 304) (To Friedrich Ritschl, April 6, 1872). After thanking Ritschl for a letter about *The Birth of Tragedy*, Nietzsche indicated that he was reassured but not completely reassured. Nietzsche then indicated that:

. . . Later it will be clearer and more evident when my book [Schrift] "On the Future of Our Educational Institutions" will be published. . . .

#208 (3, p. 308) (To Franziscka and Elizabeth Nietzsche, April 15, 1872)

. . . By the way, the result of my lectures was extraordinary – emotion, inspiration, and animosity – beautifully paired. . . .

#212 (3, pp. 313–14) (To Erwin Rohde, April 30, 1872)

. . . Indeed my 6 lectures will now still not be published, rather first next winter after a complete reworking. . . .

#220 (3, p. 323) (To Erwin Rohde, May 12, 1872)

. . . By the way I want to bring with for you my winter lectures, through which I have called forth here an incommensurable excitement and inspiration, especially among the students. They will not be published . . . .

#246 (4, p. 39) (To Richard Wagner, July 25, 1872)

At the beginning of next Winter I will still hold my Basel lectures, the sixth and seventh, "On the Future of Educational Institutions." I, at least, want to become *ready*, even in the downwardly disposed and lower form, in which I have treated that theme up till now. For the *higher* treatment I must become even "riper" and must seek to educate [bilden] myself – oh, such a good intention! But what can I, so alone, achieve! Sometime or other I must flee to Bayreuth, to your vicinity, as the true "educational institution" . . . .

#248 (4, p. 42) (to Carl von Gersdorff, August 2, 1872)

I myself am reworking my lectures on education.

#249 (4, p. 43) (To Erwin Rohde, August 2, 1872)

I am about to rework the lectures on education. Give me a little word about that – for you must know that I have no judgment regarding them and would gladly allow myself to be instructed. . . .

#270 (4, p. 83) (To Malwida von Meysenbug, November 7, 1872). Nietzsche sent Malwida the five lectures and said of them:

Read this indeed with a wholly determined and indeed Basel public in mind; it would now appear to me impossible to allow such a thing to be published, for it does not go enough into the depths and is dressed up in a farce whose invention is quite inferior.

#277 (4, p. 97) (To Erwin Rohde, December 7, 1872)

In Florentine society they are now reading my lectures on education – there appears to be there now precisely a great activity in reform plans for institutions, and it delights me very much to think that my little voice is heard in among the Italian chorus. . . .

#279 (4, p. 101) (To Carl von Gersdorff, Thursday December 12, 1872)

Miss von Meysenbug (Florence via Alfieri 16) writes me that it would be a very great joy to her to see you again. She has sent me her picture and told of the impression, which my lectures on educational institutions make upon her and the other listeners. It is now precisely a very encouraging moment that these have reached Florence, since they are almost exclusively occupied there with the reform of educational systems [Erziehungswesen's] and of teaching institutions.

#282 (4, p. 104) (To Malwida von Meysenbug, December 20, 1872)

Now you will have read the lectures and have been shocked [erschreckt] how the story suddenly breaks off, after it was so long preluded and, in sincere negativis[15] and much verbosity, had prepared

15   Latin for negativity.

ever more strongly the thirst for really new thoughts and proposals. One acquires a dry throat from these lecture and in the end nothing to drink! Speaking strictly[16] what I had devised for the last lecture – a very wild [tolle][17] and colorful scene illuminating the night – was not fit for my Basel public, and it was certainly wholly well that for me the speech remains stuck in my mouth. Besides I would be quite tortured about the resumption: since I have, however, somewhat adjourned reflection on the entire field [Gebiet], perhaps for a triennium – which will be easy for me at my age – thus the last lecture will certainly never be worked out. – The whole Rhine scenery, just as everything that appears biographical, is terribly [erschrecklich] fabricated. I will be careful about amusing or not amusing the people of Basel with the truths of my life: but even the environment of Rolandseck is unclear to me in my memory in disquieting ways . . . .

#294 (4, p. 120) (To Erwin Rohde, January 31, 1873)

Fr. V. M[eysenbug] is translating my lectures on education into Italian and will then allow them to appear in Italian newspapers: they will sound still more naïve, it is heavenly. . . .

#297 (4, pp. 127–28) (To Malwida von Meysenbug, the end of February, 1873)

. . . I am astonished and delighted, most respected Miss, that my lectures have so very much found your interest, indeed your approval; but you must believe me, by my honest face, that I can make everything better in a couple of years and want to make it better. In the meantime these lectures have a hortatory significance for me myself: they remind me of a debt, or of a task, that has fallen

16 More literally, "taken precisely."
17 Or "mad" or "crazy."

precisely to me, especially now after even the master has ceremo-
niously and publicly laid it upon my shoulders. But it is no task for
so young a person, as I am; if not one must permit me to grow
indeed older or to become old. Those lectures are primitive and in
addition somewhat improvised; just believe this from me. I do not
put much stock in them,[18] especially also on account of their trap-
pings [Einkleidung]. Fritzsch was ready to publish them, but I
have sworn to allow no book to appear with respect to which I do
not possess a conscience as pure as a Seraphim. But it does not
stand thus with respect to these lectures: they should and could be
better. . . .

#301 (4, p. 139) (To Carl von Gersdorff, April 5, 1873). Von
Gersdorff had made by hand a copy of the lectures; Nietzsche
writes:

I have therewith made my thoughts and they still make me, so
often this story comes to me. It comes to me often enough. Finally
I will still one day make the sixth lecture, only with that will you
have something finished by me in your hands. . . .

18   More literally, "I do not hold much thereon."

APPENDIX B: NOTES[1]

8[57]; p. 243.[2]

General education is only a preliminary stage [Vorstadium] of communism: education will be so weakened down in this way that it can no longer bestow privilege at all. Least of all is it a means against communism. General education, i.e., barbarity, is just the presupposition of communism. Education "according to the times" [Zeitgemäße][3] degenerates here into the extreme of education "according to the moment": i.e., the raw seizing of momentary utility [Nutzens]. One only at first saw in education something that brought utility: thus one will soon exchange that which brings utility [Nutzen] with education. No longer is culture [Kultur] that task of peoples: rather luxury, fashion. To have no needs is for a people the greatest misfortune, Lasalle[4] once declared. Hence the worker's

1   All of the selections from Nietzsche's notebooks in this appendix are taken from volume seven of the *Kritische Studienausgabe* (Nachlass 1869–74). Each selection is identified by the editor's designation, which indicates the assigned number of the notebook and of the fragment (e.g., 8 [63]) and also by the page number on which the note can be found in the *Kritische Studienausgabe*. These notes are often fragmentary, oddly formatted, and ungrammatical.

2   This notebook is thought to have been written in from Winter 1870–71 to Autumn 1872.

3   More literally, "according to the measure of the times."

4   Ferdinand Lasalle (1825–1864), author and champion of the proletariat. Founder of the Allgemein Deutschen Arbeiterverein, the "General German Workers' Union." He was friendly with Karl Marx, but Lasalleanism argued that no revolution was necessary.

education union [Arbeiterbildungsvereine]: as its intention has been repeatedly described to me, to produce needs. For national economies Christ's parable of the rich glutton [Prasser] and of the poor Lazarus stand exactly in the reverse: The glutton earns Abraham's bosom.[5] – Thus the drive toward the greatest possible generalization of education has its source in a complete secularization, in a subordination of education as a means under acquisition [Erwerb], under earthly happiness coarsely understood.

Expansion [Erweiterung] in order to be able to have many *intelligent* officials. Hegelian influence.

8[58]; p. 244.

A second source is the fear in the face of *religious oppression*. Here lies at bottom the opposite fear: a complete removal from the world [Entweltlichung] through religion, as if it were the single satisfaction of the metaphysical need. Here lies at bottom the deep instinct that Christianity in its root is hostile against any culture [Kultur] and therewith is in a necessary combination with barbarity.

8[59]; p. 244.

A third source [is] the belief in the masses, unbelief in the genius. Goethe says the genius is connected with his time through a weakness.[6] The general belief turns it around that the genius owes all his strengths to the time and therewith has only his weaknesses for himself and from himself. Here a mistake is very usual: a people receives in its genius the authentic right to existence, its justification; the masses do not produce the individual; on the contrary, they strive against him. The masses are a stone block difficult

5   *Luke* 16:19–31.
6   *Elective Affinities* II, 5.

to chisel; monstrous work is necessary by the individual in order to make something resembling a human being out of it. – General education now almost as dogma. Now one must stand in line; formerly it was the time of great individuals. Now only the servant of the masses is necessary, in specie to be the servant of a party. The goal of culture: to grab onto a party and to subordinate your life to it. – They have spoken so much of folk poetry,[7] etc.: it is always the great individuals: they are often forgotten.

8[60]; pp. 244–45.

The title, which I have given my lectures, requires in any case for all an explanation, for many of my honored listeners an apology. To speak on the future of our educational institutions
   1) neither in a special sense of Basel
   2) nor in the widest generality
      rather in regard to German educational institutions, which we ourselves indeed even here enjoy –

I do not want to forecast the *future* in the sense of a haruspex, who tells the truth out of entrails and then in the presupposition that eternal nature some time once again is confirmed.[8] *When* this future comes in, I do not know: but it suffices, in the present to convince a few of the necessity of this future; in case one does not want disconsolately to twiddle one's thumbs.[9]

8[61]; p. 245.

Everything like the Sophists Plato. And indeed new universities! Acroamatic. Thus science [Wissen]!

---

7   Or "the people's poetry."
8   More literally, "is right."
9   More literally, "to lay the hands in the lap. "

All freedom in regards to Culture.

On the other hand[10] exams [Examina][11] for particular sciences [Fachwissen].

How fast is a lawyer, a doctor swallowed up! The forming [bildende] effect of "science" [Wissenschaft].

scholarship		Extension of
state servant	}	the tendency of Gymnasiums
journalist		

Therefore the impossibility of philosophy.

8[62]; pp. 245–46.

The signal

Flight in the face of the students.

German science and German culture [Bildung].

The impossibility of philosophy at the university.

Therefore also again the impossibility of a true classical education [Bildung].

Therefore separation of the university and living art.

Where a reference [Berührung][12] comes in, then the scholar mostly has already degenerated into a journalist.

Therefore independent movements must go forth from the studentry.

The "German Burschenschaft" as a corrective of the university.

The perishing of the same out of lack of culture [Unbildung] and lack[13] of leaders.

The few spheres, in which all great German properties are to be

10 The editors extrapolate here.
11 Here Nietzsche uses the Latin form "Examina."
12 This could also mean a "contact" or "touch."
13 This "lack" [Mangel] is a separate, explicit term.

found again, German music. The Orchestra.
Advent of the musicians.

8[63]; p. 246.

Measuring sticks   no classical education

no philosophy

no art

Preponderance of the *specialty trade* [Fachs]: no authentic problems of education.
Attempt at self-discipline: Awakening of the German spirit.
The philistinish dwindling of the artistic spirit of the sterile German.[14]

8[65]; pp. 246–47.

Sketch of the teacher in the Gymnasium. The circle.

There is *too much* necessary: therefore education [Ausbildung] is to be set upon something very much attainable.

From where comes the demand [Bedürfniß]?

State offices, the university, military privileges.

What can the state have for an intention?

To break the monstrous assaults through exams [Examina].

Then it breaks the monstrous pressure for utility: it uses it.

Then it wants an equal measure of education for its officials. Education and subservience.

That is something new. The state as the leader of education. With it work elements that are opposed[15] to true education: it trusts

---

14 Nietzsche makes a pun on "keusch-deutsche," more literally, "eunuch-German."

15 Reading "entgegengesetzt" for "engegengesetzt."

to[16] breadth, it breaks in many young teachers. The laughable place of classical education: the state has an interest in the "specialized" Laconic: as it in regards to philosophy promotes either only the specialized philological or the panegyrical state philosophy.

There are different means to break to pieces the mastery of education: to break that condition of spiritual aristocracy toward which our great period of poets strove.

"Pure" philologists and journalistic middling teachers [Mittellehrer].

A mass of teachers are necessary. There are methods contrived how they can associate with antiquity.

The teachers are as it were not *permitted* to associate with antiquity. Aeschylus!

The science of language.

8[66]; pp. 247–48.

The state uses the Gymnasiums, but then it must also hold them within limits.

Everything that wants to make itself independent also falls away from the Gymnasium. There [one] has been educated [erzogen] toward officialdom, here toward earning. There the intentions of the state, here the spirit of the age, as far as it brings utility [Nutzen].

On the other side the Gymnasiums do not really educate [bilden]. Therefore it is wholly honorable to go over to the Realschule.

The laughable defenses of Gymnasium studies.

They approach one another: they stand upon one line.

Gradually they will even have the same privileges.

Then they equip just for the struggle for existence.

16   Or "reckons on."

Desperation in formal education: drives toward Realschule.

This education has its limits in the spirit of the age.

The extravagant significance[17] of education.

The abstract teacher of the people: emerged from the intention of the Gymnasium teacher.

8[69]; p. 249.

Lecture 6. The necessity of *society* and for that first of all a gathering of teachers: Plato and the sophists. The turned around position of culture [Kultur].

Lecture 7. The artist stresses the everyday and the *continuous* in education. The goal cannot be high enough, the means not simple enough: speaking, walking, seeing. Union in a new art. Requirement and satisfaction. What and how little to read. Restitution of the people.

History should give exemplifications of philosophical truths, but not allegories, rather myths.

8[82]; pp. 252–53.

I. Introduction.	The reader must be calm	
	He may not similarly bring himself in between	
	He may not expect tables	
	For our education is only meant for the calm, the selfless and those who can patiently wait.	
	Sketch of the *opposite education*: that of haste.	
	The goals and sources of this education.	
II.	The "historical" sense of the present.	
III.	Marching in rank and file.	

17 More literally, "significance as a luxury."

8[83]; pp. 253–54.

Now, that it now once has been brought to the market and, to the anger of the author, anyone can take it into the hands, consider it, and evaluate it, now must I wish to be able to say of this writing, with Aristotle: it was delivered up and also again not delivered up: wherefore I designate with all honesty as the purpose of the next, introducing fragment, to frightening off and shooing away many readers and drawing in the few. Thus hear it, you many! Odi profanum vulgus et arceo.[18] Throw the book away! It is not for you and you are not for this book. Live well!

8[84]; p. 254.

A serious author, who speaks to his people about education [Bildung] and schools [Bildungsschulen], commonly hopes for a

18   Latin for "I hate the uninitiated and drive them away"; Horace, Odes III 1,1.

limitless effect into the distance and this effect half again for just such a limitless number of self-losing readers. But with this book it conducts itself otherwise, and from the front the authentic character of its presentation of the problem of education betrays itself. For if it should not fail to achieve that sustained and broad effect, thus it needs precisely *few* readers and indeed readers of a type rarer and immediately closer to being described. The more, to the contrary, this book takes hold of a non-discriminating reading[19] public, so much more dubiously [bedenklicher] may the author feel himself to be advised: he would much more seriously regret, not to have given way from his original precaution: which was precisely directed at generally holding the public at a distance from this book, and thought to make its effect dependent alone upon a private distribution to good and worthy readers of that still-to-be-described type.

8[86]; p. 254.

VI. and VII. lecture. Contrast[20] of the artist (man of letters) and of the philosopher.

The artist is degenerated. Battle.

The students remain on the side of the man of letters.

8[87]; p. 255.

I. Entertaining, at the conclusion thrilling. μελέτη δέ τοι[21] – γνῶθι σαυτόν.[22]

19 Unangelesene means more literally "non-reading-into."
20 Nietzsche uses English here.
21 The full phrase, "μελέτη δὲ τοι ἔργον ὀφέλλει," meaning "But care makes work go well" belongs to Hesiod, *Works and Days*, line 412.
22 Greek for "know thyself," this is the most famous of the inscriptions ascribed to Apollo through the oracle at Delphi.

II. The German instruction[23] as the fundament of the classical instruction.

III. Too many teachers and students. Genius.[24] οἱ πλεῖστοι κακοί.[25] Therefore the weakening of the effect of antiquity. Therefore the alliance of the state with the weakened[26] culture [Kultur]. Serious aberration.

IV. Realschule. μηδὲν ἄγαν.[27] Assault upon what was hitherto.

V. The University. μέτρον ἄριστον.[28]

VI. The degenerated man of culture and his hopes. καιρὸν γνῶθι.[29] Hasty, historical, momentarily active, not to become ripe. The press.

VII. The future school. ἐγγύη, παρὰ δ'ἄτα.[30]

8[89]; pp. 255–56.

The philosopher had finally, standing on the pentagram looking down, spoken. Now a bright glare down in the wood. We lead him toward it. Greeting. In the mean time the students erect a stack of wood. First only a private dialogue aside. "Why so late?"

23 Or "lesson."

24 Nietzsche uses Latin here.

25 Greek for "Most [men – ἀνθρωποί] are bad." This phrase is historically ascribed to Bias of Priene, one of the Seven Wise Men of Greek antiquity.

26 The editors interpolate the end of this word.

27 Greek for "Nothing too much." This is another of the famous inscriptions found at the temple of Apollo at Delphi. It is some times ascribed to the temple of Zeus at Olympia.

28 Greek for "Measure is best." This was historically a favorite saying of the philosopher Cleobulus.

29 Greek for "Know your opportunity." This is a saying historically ascribed to Pittacus, another some times counted among the Seven Wise Men.

30 Greek meaning "Give security and a bane is alongside." This saying also is attributed as a Delphic inscription. See Plato, *Charmides*, 165a.

The just-performed [gehabte] triumph – explanation. The philosopher sad: he does not believe in this triumph and presupposes an obligation [Zwang] in the other to which he must yield. For *us* indeed here there is probably no illusion?[31] He reminds of their youthful agreement. The other betrays himself as converted, as a realist. Ever greater disillusionment[32] of the philosopher. The students call the other to the flaming stack of wood in order to speak. He talks about the German spirit now. (Popularization, press, self-sufficiency, in rank and file, historical, work for posterity (not to become ripe), the German scholar as the flower. Natural science.)

"You lie" vehement reply of the philosopher. The difference between the German and the pseudo-German.[33] Haste, unripe, journalist, cultured lectures, no society, the hope of natural science. The significance of history. Mocking consciousness of victory – we the victors, all education [Erziehung] serves us, every national excitation[34] serves us (the university of Strassburg). A mockery of the time of Schiller-Goethe.

Protest against the exploitation of great national excitations: no new universities. But the more that spirit prevails and the invading barbarity, so much more securely will the most powerful [Kräftigsten] natures be pushed by the camp,[35] compelled toward union. Sketch of the future of this union. Heavy sigh: whence the point of departure? Description of the kernel of hope. The stack of wood collapses. He calls: Hail this wish. Midnight bell.

Counter reply: Curse this wish.

Mocking withdrawal of the students, pereat diabolus atque irrisores.[36]

Painful renunciation of the old friend.

31 Täuschung could mean "deception."
32 Enttäuschung.
33 Afterdeutsch contains an anatomical reference to the "aft" portion of the body.
34 Erregung might be translated as "movement."
35 More literally, "side.'
36 The last and third-to-last lines of a verse of the German student song

8[91]; p. 257.

Preface
The characteristic courses of the present education.
Institutions for the necessities of life,
The Gymnasium.
Too many teachers.
The University.
New foundation in Strassburg.
The age of wars, thus it is a duty to think upon *better* explosions of patriotic emotions.

8[92]; pp. 257–58.

A. What is education?
The purpose of education.
Appreciation and promotion of its noblest contemporaries.
Preparation of those becoming and those coming.
Education can only apply to that which is to be formed [bilden].
Not to an intelligible character.
The task of education: to live and *to work* in the noblest endeavors of its people or of the human being.
Thus not only to receive[37] and to learn, rather to live.

"Gaudeamus igitur" ("Let us rejoice"); cf. *Human, All Too Human: Assorted Opinions and Maxims*, 339. This song stems from the sixteenth century and is the most famous song of German student life. The line between the lines Nietzsche quotes is "Quivis antiburschius." The lines quoted by Nietzsche mean "Let perish the devil, together with those who mock!" The line omitted means "whomever is against the Bursch," meaning literally "against the youth," but perhaps coming to mean "against the Burschenschaft."

37 Nietzsche conjugates a Latin word here according to German rules.

To free its time and its people from spoiled lines, to have its ideal image before the eyes.

The purpose of history, to hold firm this image [Bild].

Philosophy and art: history is a means.

To perpetuate the highest spirits: culture is the immortality of the noblest spirits.

Monstrous wrestling with necessity – culture as transforming power.

Throughout to be understood *productively*.

The judgment of the human being depends throughout also on education.

The task of the educated, to be *truthful* and really to place themselves in a relationship to everything great.

Education is life in the sense of great spirits with purposes of great goals.

To step out: the consideration of Goethe from the standpoint of the educated and from that of the uneducated scholars.

Or

Schopenhauer.

Appreciation[38] *for greatness* and *fruit bearing.*

To recognize in every human being the good and the great and the hatred against everything halfway and weak.

To live among[39] the constellations: *fame turned around*: that consists in living on among the noblest feelings of the world to come after [Nachwelt]: culture in living on among the noblest feelings of the world that came before [Vorwelt]. The *non-transitoriness* of the great and the good.

The transitoriness of the human being and culture. The most important advances of the human being as such are to be drained off from its relationship to the whole stream of later generations.

38 Or "Understanding."
39 Or "under."

8[93]; pp. 258–59.

I. *The character of the present education.*
   2) Haste and not-becoming ripe
   2) The historical, not wanting to live, the swallowing up of the hardly born present. The copying. Literary history.
   3) The paper world. Senseless writing and reading.
   4) In rank and file. Disinclination toward the genius. The "sociale"[40] human being. – Socialism.
   5) The courante[41] human being.
   6) The specialized scholar. To live better, not to know more.
   7) Lack of serious philosophy.
   8) Atrophy of art. "Reichstag[42] education."
   9) The new concept of the "German."

II. *The schools under the effect of this education.*

III. It lacks the next thing, planting[43] education through everyday habituation
   Exotic character of all education (e.g., gymnastic exercise).
   It lacks the guidance and the tribunal of education.
   It lacks the artistic overwhelming.
   The serious consideration of the world as the singular salvation in the face of socialism.
   New education [Erziehung] necessary, not new universities. Strassburg.
   Restoration[44] of the true German spirit.

40   French for "social."
41   French for "current."
42   The Imperial Diet.
43   Pflanzenden has been rendered as "cultivating" elsewhere.
44   Or "production."

IV. Proposal from the convocation of a perennial[45] pedagogical brotherhood, be it from its own means, be it that a state should be insightful enough. These should not, so to speak, report; rather first learn among themselves and reciprocally attach themselves.

Nothing is to be done for the present with better salaries: generally everything remains palliative.

Education [Erziehung] through music.

8[97]; p. 260.

To observe [nachleben] greatness, in order for it to set an example [vorzuleben]. Everything depends upon the fact that greatness is rightly taught. Therein rests educating [Bilden].

That is the measuring stick with which our time is to be measured.

8[98]; pp. 260–61.

His own noble feeling stretched out in space and time to participate in the great enlightenment of all. This the eudaimonism of the best

Is ennoblement possible?

The intelligible character is unchangeable: but that is practically wholly indifferent. For those original qualities of the individual we can never grasp: first a mass of interpretations shoved in between color these qualities as good and evil. This world of interpretation is, however, very much to be determined. Habituation the most important of all.

Ennoblement through the growing elevation of the goal.

45   Or "of many years."

8[99]; p. 261.

Gross error, to take the eternal individual as something wholly separate. Its after-effects go into eternity, as it is the result of countless generations.

It is culture, that those noblest moments of all generations
almost forms [bilden] a continuum, in which one can live further.

For each individual, culture is that it has a continuum of knowledges and noblest thoughts and lives further in them.

A degree of culture (deeds of love and the sacrifice of everything common).

One such feeling of *love* blazes up at the highest knowledges,
even with the artist.

Fame.

8[101]; pp. 261–62.

    I. Introduction. General matters.
    II. The Gymnasium, the German instruction, classical.
    III. Excesses and the grounds.
    IV. Repercussions upon the other institutions.
    V. The university: science and education.
    VI. Proposals and conclusion.

8[102]; p. 262.

The Gymnasiums lead over into the Realschulen.
The university into technical schools.[46]
The elementary schools [Volksschulen] as a thing of the community.
The philosophical faculties to be detached.

46   Fachschule. Fach and words containing it have been translated as "specialized" elsewhere.

8[103]; p. 262.

The scene before the last: how the individual must educate [bilden] himself. Hermitage. Battle. An explanation. How possible alone?

Two masters.

The last scene as anticipation of the future institution. The flame purifies itself from the smoke. "Pereat diabolus atque irrisores."[47]

8[105]; p. 263.

Deviation of the Gymnasium.
1) The true goal of the Gymnasium, the Realschulen. Consequence of the Gymnasium now.
2) The elementary schools [Volksschulen] – the teacher. Error of the goal of the Gymnasium now.
3) The university – subjection under the state and earning a living.
4) Hopes.

8[106]; p. 263.

Disbelief, that the institutions are solid –
Over all the contradiction of the alleged tendency and of reality. To be demonstrated in the Gymnasium (most highly determining for the others). Consideration of the results of the Gymnasium (antiquity, culture, German work. Alienation from art. The teacher and his preparation).

47 Nietzsche's text lacks the final quotation marks. For the Latin quotation see footnote 36.

Scholarly method – schools, forms [Bänke], etc. Alienation from art. Classical education. The teacher.

The slavery of the state. Because all tendencies are merely pretended, the Gymnasium has got into slavery to the state.

Verifications – the scholars or the journalists.

The true goal – an arsenal for the battle with the present.

8[107]; pp. 263–64.

I. Superiority of the "Gymnasiums," the running wild of educational tasks, the "people" as judge of the intellectuals, the task of the Realschule – to prepare for the struggle for life.
II. The running wild of the teacher. Repercussions in the elementary school, abstract education [Erziehung].
III. The exploitation of general education by the state.
IV. Hopes.

8[108]; p. 264.

We had already become restless at the last part of that speech through which the gray philosopher instructed us about the essence of the university, and had at any moment a sudden interruption of his speech –

8[113]; p. 266.

Educational Institutions and their Fruits

Culture [Kultur] lacks an *imperative public authority*. Even Goethe stood eternally alone. Thus one circle can emancipate itself from the university, another from the Gymnasium. Reverence for the real, as the opposite to the discipline of the classical: indeed the real is gradually transmitted into bourgeoisery [Spießbürgerei] and the low German (the greatest commonality is naturally a common dialect).

Gutzkow as a degenerated Gymnasiast.

Young Germany as run away students.

Julian Schmidt, Freytag, Auerbach. Opposition against the imperative world of the beautiful and the elevated[48]: protest of photography against the painting. The "Roman." Thereby in them after effects of the romantic reverence for the German: but false and idealistic.

Mommsen (Cicero).[49] Fastening of scholarship to the political daily routine.

Jahn[50] and Grenzboten[51]

Diesterweg[52] and the abstract teacher.

(To remodel my dialogue artistically.)

8[118]; p. 267.

Even the introduction, honored listeners, is marked; therewith the whole has quite nothing of the *accountant* [Buchmäßiges]. Only remembrances. Everything should remind of the personal.

9[53][62]; pp. 297–98.

Fundamental considerations:
Why the division of the peoples – and the scholars instruction?

48 Or "the sublime."
49 Theodor Mommsen (1817–1903), famous historian. His masterpiece was *The History of Rome*. He had the reputation of having glorified non-democratic men like Caesar and having disparaged the virtues of Cicero.
50 Otto Jahn (1813–1869), German archaeologist, philologist, and writer on art and music. He taught Mommsen. He took part in the political movements of 1848–49.
51 Name of weekly paper, *Border Messages*, formed on the German border.
52 Adolph Diesterweg (1790–1866). An influential pedagogue and promoter of the Volksschule system.
53 The notebook labeled "9" is thought to have been written in during 1871.

When does it happen? – at the wrong[54] time, where one does not know the natures.

Because the claim to culture of the Gymnasium is a *lie*.
The standards of the compelled ones have fully brought it low. Originally there are indeed only schools for scholars; but no schools for culture.

Scholarship and culture do not hang together with one another.

"General" education degrades exceptional "education" as such. The journalist is a necessary reaction: a spawn of the so-called general education – : "The common human being with the all too common[55] education."

9[63]; p. 298.

On the Future of Our Educational Institutions
1. Education as an exceptio.[56] On the concept of an educational institution.
2. The Gymnasium: at bottom a specialized school: in the service of a vocation.
3. The Volksschule: the journalist and the Volksschule teacher.
4. The Realschule: at bottom a specialized school: in the service of a vocation.
5. The teacher.
6. Proposals (against socialism).

9[64]; p. 298.

Against the striving after "general[57] education": much more to seek after truer, deeper, and rarer education, thus after the *narrowing*

54 More literally, "non-right."
55 "Allgemeine" is translated as "general" above. The word translated as "common" is "gemeine."
56 Latin for "exception."
57 Allgemein.

and concentration of education: as a counter-weight against the journalists.

The division of labor of science and the specialized school leads now toward the narrowing of education. Up till now in all things education has only become *worse*. The human being become finished[58] is wholly abnormal. The factory rules. The human being becomes a cog.[59] – The main motive for the generalization of education is fear in the face of religious pressure.

9[65]; p. 299.

Otto Jahn: infamous manner, the attempt, with the wholly empty heartlessness of his Grenzboten "Enlightenment,"[60] to rivet deeply thinking and deeply living images of the world to his wooden peg.

9[69]; p. 299.

Socialism is a result of general non-culture [Unbildung], abstract education [Erziehung], crudeness of feeling [Gemüthsroheit]. With a certain height of affluence, "ostracism."

"Education" must be, as recompense and sanction, the protective agency of all the oppressed.

9[70]; pp. 299–301.

On the Future of Our Educational Institutions.
Sameness of the instruction for all up until the 15th year.
For the pre-destination to the Gymnasium through the parents and so on is an injustice.

58 Or "ready," or "capable," or "mature."
59 More literally, "a screw."
60 More literally, Aufklärung means "clearing up. "

Volks- and Gymnasium-teacher is a senseless division.

Then *specialized schools.*

Finally schools of education [Bildungsschulen] (20.–30. year) for the education of teachers.

The regular errors of the method now.

1) False concept of classical education.

2) The incapacity of Gymnasium teachers.

3) The impossibility of such a general educational institution as the Gymnasiums now *appear* to be.

4) *Military service* is permitted to make no division. Before all the greedy demand of the industrials is to be broken.

5) The terrible concept of the Volks teachers and elementary [Elementar] teachers.

The authentic *calling*[61] *of the teacher*, the teacher's status is to be *broken*. Giving instructions is a duty of old men.

The result: a monstrous mass of education is discovered. The demand for the *specialist* is more generally and more satisfyingly executed so that the isolated individuals are not spoiled in an excess of burdens.

A true spiritual aristocracy was summoned.

To make the *beginning* with *educational institutions for teachers.*

The universities are to be transformed from scholarly institutions into specialized institutions.

A spiritual aristocracy is created.

Classical instruction is generally only fruitful for a small number.

The "Realschule" has a wholly excellent kernel. One should compel no one toward education. To decide for it oneself one must be *older.*

One must decide oneself toward *education* from out of the specialized school.

The *teachers of a specialized school* are scientific *masters*, who

---

61   Or "vocation."

(after they have made it through the time of education) have turned back to the speciality.

Instruction by old men should preserve the tradition.

14^{62}[10]; p. 378.

On the Future
of Our
Educational Institutions

Notes. Autumn 71.

14[11]; pp. 378–79.

Education.

Narrowing necessary, in opposition to the striving after expansion. In this striving *after expansion* lies at bottom [the following]

   1) The optimism of the national economy – as much knowledge as possible – as much production as possible – as much happiness as possible

   2) Fear in the face of religious oppression

   3) Belief in the masses, disbelief in the genius.

[The following] works against this striving, for *diminution*

   1) The division of labor, even for science

   2) The different churches

   3) Fear in the face of socialism as a fruit of that optimism

Our standpoint is that of the *narrowing* and concentration, thus *strengthening* (against 2.) and *narrowing* (against 1.)

Here *nature* speaks her word.

62 The notebook labeled "14" is thought to have been written in from the early part of 1871 until the beginning of 1872.

Those are *strivings*, these are *truths*.

All of our *educational institutions* (which have emerged out of these strivings) are to be measured in this *original truth*.

But the *value* [Geltung] of the *truth* is a very different thing to [different] times: those principles lying at the bottom of the strivings also lay claim to truth and thus *cover over* the truth.

Both strivings, as *maxims of education* [Erziehungsmaximen], can of all things have the *result*, to push down the *level* of the spiritual aristocracy and to diminish its influence.

For even the born aristocracy of the spirit must have an education [Erziehung] and value [Geltung] appropriate to it. The correct educational principle [Erziehungsprincip] can only be to bring the greater mass into the right relationship to the *spiritual aristocracy*: that is the authentic *task of culture* (according to the three Hesiodic possibilities); *the organization of the genius state – that is the true Platonic republic.*

14[12]; pp. 379–80.

I mean *ethical and intellectual education.*

The manifestations of ethical education are very different, according to the intellectual background.

Education in the service of the state.

Education in the service of society.

Education in the service of acquisition [Erwerbs].

Education in the service of science.

Education in the service of the church.

From these unnatural subordinations result *two directions*: expansion and diminution

Common is the *disbelief in the genius*: whereby their *unnaturalness* betrays itself: just so a great optimism.

14[13]; p. 380.

1. To complete[63] the genius through education, to make smooth the path
2. To make possible his activities[64]
3. To find him out

From out of the standpoint of the non-genius:
1. To learn obedience and humility (Hesiod.)
2. Correct recognition of the narrowness of every vocation.
3. To collect material for the genius.

14[14]; p. 380.

"Organization of the intellectual caste" the eternal task of education, independent from the momentary church and state.

14[15]; pp. 380–81.

Classical Education

The highest education [is] something completely *useless*: the privilege of genius. Out of his education one can make no *life's vocation*, from which to live. This is the idea[65] of the wise man of Socrates, who took no money.

The scholar in the place of the educated man [Gebildeten]   } Recognition marks of the *Middle Ages*.
The teacher by vocation in the place of the model wise man

---

63 Or "perfect."
64 Or "effects."

Our scholars have been arranged according to this medieval principle. The education of one particular *class of teacher* has been the result.

Practically anyone can become a scholar, but few an educated man [Gebildeter]. *The generality of scholarship* – the old goal of education. To drill as many as possible into scholars – the highest old task of education [Erziehungsaufgabe]. Life under the slavery of *science*.

From out of that emerged the *Latin school*, the *non-national* school for the education of scholars.

The demand for *classical education* is something wholly modern and an inversion[66] of the tendency of the Gymnasium.

In the mean time it is evident that one does not need to come from Latin to science, equally so that the scholar and the educated man [Gebildete] are not identical.

Now a bold move:[67] the old Gymnasium is recast[68] into the *formal school*.

Great *public lie*. The old are truly in a still-higher degree our true masters and teachers: but not for youngsters.

Our Gymnasium teachers (our best) are not as it were prepared[69] for this demand. They educate [erziehen] accordingly as before scholars, but authentically still only philologists.

If one wants to be honest, one must at some time transform the Gymnasium into a philological-historical specialty institution in the service of science.

14[16]; pp. 381–82.

The more highly a human being is educated [gebildet], so

65   Or "representation."
66   Or "perversion."
67   More literally a "hold," as in wrestling.
68   Or "recoined."
69   "Eingerichtet" is translated as "arranged" above.

much lonelier is he: i.e., he has intercourse with the great of all time, and this illustrious society makes him somewhat cautious. He is not "courant."

14[18]; p. 382.

The exams [Examina] with their abundance of intellectual demands are a guarantee for the *ethical* conquest of an immense mass in the service of a future state position. Whoever shows himself submissive here is already marked.

14[20]; pp. 382–83.

The Realschule

The *name* is a protest against the alleged formal school of the modern Gymnasium.

According to the essence it is in the mean time still a medley that seeks to fill out the monstrous gap that the Gymnasium leaves. With the monstrous greatness of the domain, which it wants to span, it has been compelled to remain something altogether common, and becomes thus practically again *formal*.

Not the Realschule, but an immense number of specialized schools, must step into the gaps and indeed as well vocational schools as schools for scholars. Their appearance is therefore a great necessity and a sign that the old Gymnasium is *recognized*.

The indistinctness of form still shows in the mean time how young the thought is. There are mostly dull mirror images of the Gymnasium.

This shows itself especially with the similar[70] demands to be a military school and preparatory institution for university.

The university and the Gymnasium have a common soil: the university and the Realschule do not. Therefore this one must, if it

70   Or "same."

thinks in terms of consequences,[71] deny the sole mastery of the university.

The polytechnic is something that relates similarly to the university, as the Realschule to the Gymnasium.

Young, still unripe. An uncounted number of forms or polytechnics, i.e., scientific specialized schools, are necessary. Now overall *formal* education is still stressed too much: from an altogether too-great commonness.

Against the formal education justified objections:
The Realschule contests the sole mastery of the Gymnasium for the paths of education.
Whether the real knowing[72] will thus have good teachers?
The Realschule does not want to be a specialty school: but yet [wants] to have the direct kinds of vocation closer to its focus.[73]
Everything can at one time become *useful*: an important thought!

14[21]; p. 383.

The Volksschule

The abstract teacher.
The separation of society.
The use of the church.

14[23]; p. 384.

The Teacher

The absolute teacher – the status of the teacher.
The influence of the state.

71   "Consequent" is not a German word.
72   Or "real science."
73   More literally, "closer in the eye."

The exam[74] – because of the state. Signs of submission.

Emancipation of the teacher from the state.

The educated [gebildete] people's army – a melancholy concept.

The privileges of the examined ones with the military.

Through examinations [Examina] and antiquity[75] one holds the ambitious in the state in a bridle.

14[24]; p. 384.

The University

As a state institution degenerated.

The academy.

Nourishment – and subsistence – institution.

As the highest counter power against the state it is wholly used up and annihilated.

14[25]; pp. 384–85.

The Results

Our schools hint at a still-much-greater *division of work*. *Full education* is hence striven after ever more seldomly: there is no school that sets itself this task. Yes, one does not know what to do,[76] if one seeks after teaching material for this full education.

Hence the power of the binding, altogether common human being of the *journalist* may for a time become still ever greater: they unite the most different spheres: wherein their essence and their task lies.

74   Here Nietzsche uses the German word "Examen."
75   Here Nietzsche uses the word "Anciennität."
76   More literally, "one does not know counsel."

Thus in order to become stronger the *full human being* must once again elevate himself, not as a means for all circles, rather as the *leader* of the movement. For this leader there is now no organization. It would be thinkable, a school of the noblest men, purely useless, without demands, an areopagus[77] for justice [Justiz] of the spirit, – but these human beings of education may not be young. They must live as models: as the authentic educational authorities [Erziehungsbehörden].[78]

This highest education I recognize up till now only as a reawakening of *Greekdom*.[79] Battle against civilization.

By this forum must be distinguished what limits generally the advancement of science has:

The *authentic passion for knowing* is of all things weakened by the division of work.

According to both ends essentially new organizations are necessary: for the education of children [Kindererziehung] removal of the abstract teacherdom; for the highest education [Erziehung] the possibility of a living together. In the middle will the development of their way go. An elementary-school teacher caste [Volkslehrerstand] is wholly of evil [Übel]. The *teaching of children is a parental- and community-duty*: Upholding of the tradition is the main task. In the heights a great free look. Both are probably compatible.[80]

This spiritual aristocracy must also make for itself freedom from the *state*; which now holds science fenced in.[81]

---

77 Areopagus is Greek for "hill of Ares." It is a high, rocky hill northwest of the Acropolis in Athens. It was the sacred meeting place of the council of elders, also bearing the name Areopagus. This council originally bore significant legislative and judicial powers and was associated with aristocracy.

78 "Behörde" is translated above as "agency."

79 More literally, "Hellenedom."

80 Or "can tolerate it."

81 The *Kritische Studienausgabe* has "in Zaune," if "in Zaume" is read then the state holds science "in a bridle" as in 14[23].

14[26]; p. 385.

The Foundations of the New Education

Not historical; rather living in the moment.[82]
The "divine one-sidednesses."

18[83][2]; pp. 411–12.

I. *Introduction.*
   The title.
   Not special Basel relationship.
   No responsibility for useful applications.
   The place in which one *does* so much and probably even correspondingly *thinks*. *To remind*, not to instruct.
   Equally as little from out of the horizon of all people of culture [Kulturvölker].
   Much more the *German* institutions, Volksschule, Gymnasium, University.
   They tie us to our past.
   Dubious innovations [Neuerungen] of the modern, contemporary spirit.
   In regard to their future all hope lies in a renovation [Erneuerung] of the German spirit.
   Important for our theme, to understand again the original sense without its modern degenerations.
   Thus neither for the "self-evident ones."[84]
   nor for the despairing ones.

82 "Hinein leben" means taking it easy or happy-go-lucky living.
83 The notebook labeled "18" is thought to have been written in from the end of 1871 until the early part of 1872.
84 More literally, "self-understood ones."

Rather for[85] the struggling ones, whose image [Bild] as it were
is Schiller.

Main part. No definition of education.

It depends upon the *last goal* in whose service the
education is put.

We foresee[86] from the phraseology of education as
an "end in itself."

II. If we want to rubricate[87] the education goals of our time, thus
we find

Education in the service   of acquisition
                             of sociability
                             of the state
                             of the church
                             of science.

Two directions are permitted:[88]

1. *The most possible expansion*
Optimism of the national economy
Hegel's exaggerated concept of the state.
Also society.
2. *Diminution, weakening,* some times inten-
tionally, some times unintentionally
Division of labor
Different churches'
Fear in the face of socialism.

85   This is interpolated by the editors of the *Kritische Studienausgabe.*
86   The text has sehen, "see"; the editors of the *Kritische Studienausgabe*
     interpolate absehen, "foresee."
87   To rubricate is a printer's term meaning to print a heading in a dif-
     ferent color.
88   More literally, "go through."

Both directions have something *unnatural*: the disbelief in[89] the *intellectual* pyramid, in the *genius*, i.e., *aversions*[90] against *strengthening* and *narrowing*.

18[3]; p. 413.

The intention of nature to come to *completion*.[91] The genius is insofar timeless. The goal is always reached.

The goal of *education* is the propping up of nature for this timeless completion: somewhat as medicine is the propping up of nature's striving for health.

The recognition mark of this highest education is *uselessness* from the standpoint of egoism, or timeliness.

In exchange a people gains through its geniuses the right to existence: the highest *use*.

The task of education: To complete the genius, to smooth his courses, to make possible his activities [Wirken] through reverence, to find him out.[92]

Therewith had been longed for from the non-genius, as an education goal

1. Obedience and modesty
2. Correct recognition of the narrowness of every vocation
3. Serviceability for the genius, to collect material.

The whole "organization of the intellectual castes." Therewith a midwife service for the birth of the genius. Highest and difficult work!

The three Hesiodic possibilities.

89 This is interpolated by the editors of the *Kritische Studienausgabe*.
90 More literally, "counter-wills."
91 Or "perfection."
92 Cf. the note for 14[13].

Special: resumption of the reawakening of antiquity, thus the reformation movement.

18[5]; p. 414.

1. Scenery. Introduction. Pistols. (Duel.)
2. Gymnasium.
3. Realschule.
4. Volksschule.
5. University.
6. The "shedding."[93] Shooting star. Pistols. Laughter. Battle in the cave. Dream of the future.

18[6]; p. 414.

Two friends. Become familiar at Rolandseck. Promise, to be there once every year. Precisely in connection with this day. Much trouble, undone.

18[10]; p. 415.

On the Future
of Our Educational Institutions.
Six public lectures
By
F. N.

Beginning of the year 1872.

93   Of the skin, like a snake.

18[11]; p. 415.

First lecture	January 16th
Second lecture	February 6th
Third lecture	February 27th
Fourth lecture	March 5th
Fifth lecture	March 23rd
Sixth lecture	

First speech held on the sixteenth of January.
Second speech held on the sixth of February.

APPENDIX C: SCHOOL ESSAY[1]

Character portrait of Cassius from Julius Caesar[2]
(School Essay May 1863)

Brutus and Cassius are through and through not characters of the same kind; their difference conditions to a certain extent their decline. The placing together, however, of exactly these two natures, which so to speak complement each other, but to whose individual defects the ill will of circumstances clings, manifests on the one hand the deep glimpse of the poet into the law of elective affinity, on the other hand his bold artistic grasp that chose exactly these two characters in order to show in them the two different motives in their reciprocal action that were active in the assassination

1   This school essay is included here, in part, as an example of the kind of assignment about which the old philosopher complains in the second lecture as being inappropriate for the young. Nietzsche wrote it when he was eighteen. At that age Nietzsche focused on Cassius and on the nature and limitations of friendship. This can be fruitfully compared with Nietzsche's later reading of *Julius Caesar*, in *Gay Science*, section 98. There Nietzsche calls *Julius Caesar* Shakespeare's "best tragedy," and Nietzsche interprets the play as being primarily concerned with philosophic independence.

2   This is a translation of a school essay that Nietzsche wrote while at Schulpforta. It is based upon the text found in volume I of the Musarion edition of Nietzsche's *Gesammelte Werke*, pp.113–21; all footnotes were added by the translator; all references, unless otherwise noted, are to Shakespeare's *Julius Caesar*.

of Caesar. It is namely with Brutus essentially the hatred against all mastery of volition, the inborn, old Roman sense for freedom, which lets him "sacrifice" his most beloved, just as ignoble and selfish motives predominate in most of the souls of his fellow-conspirators: even so in Cassius, who appears always to vacillate whether he hates tyrants more than tyranny. Surely he hates both, but the oppressive feeling of standing opposite a higher and more grandiose personality, of wandering between the giant legs of this colossus, therewith the consciousness of a greater bodily force, the memory of Caesar's weakness: all of that lures his choleric heart to implacable resentment. He it is indeed, who introduces the conspiracy; he is the right man for the formation and instigation of conspirators. His exterior allows his never-resting soul to show through: a hollow, hungry look, a haggard form, nevertheless the strength and muscularity of his limbs, which were hardened in war, sharp ear and sharp eye, a bitter and infrequent smile in the most rigid tensions, which appears to despise the spirit that can still smile. He sleeps little at night, he reads much and observes with delicacy, he despises the pleasures of life, does not play, is no friend of music, chats not with the drunk and fraternizes not with every man. These hints about his essence are given to us partially by him himself, partially by Caesar, who sees through and fears him, yes who fears almost him alone. There are still more external traits, merely the forms of his spirit. But his inner nature we read out of his actions, especially out of his relations with Brutus.

Cassius asks Brutus along to view the proceedings of the race; he wants perhaps to wake his thoughts through the spectacle. Brutus refuses, but he does not want to hinder Cassius if he should want to watch. Cassius takes this and his whole manner of late for strange and stubborn and concludes from this a lessening of Brutus's love. It is certain that a similar manner of Cassius would really have its ground in a diminution of his love; for the views which Cassius has of friendship are so nobly and highly strained that we are entitled to this conclusion. There is this atoning trait in his nature, with so many repulsive and, especially at first glance, offensive things, this deep and elevated love of friends.

Cassius seeks now, since Brutus does not want to attend the spectacle where Caesar is supposed to put on the crown, himself to lead him to his own thoughts; he hears from him that stirrings of a fighting nature have tortured him of late. The way that Cassius goes now is very careful; he calls Brutus to seek himself in his inner self and considers himself as a mirror for the eye of the friend wherein this one should see his own worth. Honor is the content of his speech, since he has recognized a living feeling for honor as especially powerful in Brutus. He would rather not be there than in fear before a being as he himself is, before a being that, although weaker according to nature, has become a God and yet merely negligently nods toward him. Cassius does not recognize the elevated spirit of Caesar; he wants rather to measure power according to bodily strength and despises a human being who trembles and whimpers with a fever like a sick girl. However, that such a man can bestride the world like a colossus, that would be precisely the fault of the enervated and effeminant Rome, that would be its fault, not that of destiny: Caesar could not be the wolf if the Romans had not become sheep.

Cassius reached his goal; three-quarters of Brutus he already made his own in this thing; the thoughts excited by him dig and nibble away in the breast of his friend.

Later as Casca sketches a picture of how Caesar refused the crown three times, there are the two questions of Cassius, typical of his sharp-sighted and statesman-like spirit: "Who offered the crown?"[3] and then: "What did Cicero say thereto?"[4] The latter matters much to him as an honorable man who, as a supporter of the conspiracy, would take from it the appearance of youthful enthusiasm.

In order to drive Brutus forward in the given way, he shies away from no means; no moralistic doubts are felt as he is determined, by means of thrown-in notes, to shake up Brutus. It is a harder material out of which the nature and conscience of Cassius is

3   I. ii, 232.
4   I. ii, 278.

formed, but this material is solid and genuine and does not falter under the pressure of circumstances. In him walk political and anthropological slyness and a direct and old Roman sense next to one another, almost without touching and fighting, which would stamp the impression of instability on his character. His passion, his hatred against Caesar holds these different qualities apart from one another.

A proof for that is his following conversation with Casca, whom he seizes by his superstition in a highly dexterous way. As he sees that this one would be awakened thereby out of his dull [stumpfen] repose, he compares his own work with that fiery and fearsome night. He knows how to draw sparks from the crude man by interrupting him suddenly:

> "But, O my grief!
> Where hast thou led me? I perhaps speak this
> before a willing bondsman?"[5]

He speaks with fire and strength, his whole heart turns round when he speaks of Caesar and the womanly sentiment of the people. And indeed he appears nevertheless always sharply conscious of the means by which he might fetter individual minds. Even how necessary Brutus and his recognized sense of nobility may be for the whole conspiracy, necessary for political reasons, for reasons of self-interest, he recognized that deeply and confirmed it even in front of Casca. With the decided ones among the conspirators he makes few suggestions, but always of the highest practicality: he wants that they take an oath among one another; he asks "But how with Cicero? Has anyone inquired after him?"[6] Throughout he confronts Brutus and indeed not with practical considerations; rather with ideal enthusiasm for his good work that should be desecrated by nothing. Although in the respect that Cassius wants to have Antony murdered at the same time with Caesar – surely a desire justified in the highest given the need – Cassius steps back, even

5   I. iii, 111–13.
6   II. i, 141.

if grudgingly; he may recognize that herein rests destruction; he gauges fully the importance of this political sin, but in the face of Brutus he is no longer Cassius or at least not the same Cassius as he shows himself to the others. He who bows before no one cannot offer resistance to the superior moral greatness of his friend, he notices, as his practical reasons and considerations grow pale before this light, and, after he has led Brutus astray into a monstrous error, he drags this one along into destruction, not willingly and consciously, but nevertheless he abandons the standpoint from which he alone can still ward off the difficult consequences of this error.

Before and during the deed he is generally restless, spying out the precarious, pushing opposition to the side, like the soothsayer Artemidorus, prepared for the most terrible, with dagger in hand in order to use it against Caesar or turn it against himself. Behind the speaker's platform he crowds together the conspirators, inquires after Antony, praises the deed and its authors, calls Brutus to speak and seeks to win Antony through dignities for him, because he knows that Brutus wants to let him live. However, as this adaptable and richly endowed friend of Caesar wants to speak to the people, there Cassius takes Brutus to the side: "You do not know what you do! Who knows what will occur! I am not for it."[7] Again he divines with a correct glimpse, as here their destruction approaches. And again he gives way, because Brutus does not want to hear of it.

The drama nears its ending. Unhappiness pursues the murderers of Caesar; it negated Brutus's ideal dreams and disposed him to be dark and gloomy; it did not weigh down Cassius, who with the same adaptability knows how to find himself in his situation, and, again, shies away from no means in order to make it endurable. Not to Brutus' pleasure; the irritation caused thereby calls forth a highly passionate scene between them, in which both express themselves harshly and insultingly. In this scene the drama peaks; both natures, led to the most extreme, reveal their ownmost essence, which community and art usually cover over. Cassius loses his

---

7   III. i, 232–44. Some of Cassius' lines and an intervening speech of Brutus are omitted.

entire hold on this world as he sees himself treated thus; he breaks down, this strong character, as the single sweetness of this existence, his friend, appears lost to him. "One watches all my faults, he proclaims them however crushing, marks them down in a notebook, learns them by heart, throws them in my teeth."[8] His heart "richer than Pluto's mine, worth more than gold,"[9] he offers to his one-time friend. And that is no overdoing of the moment; the genuinely human is in his character a root indeed deeply buried, but all the more powerful and rich in sap. His love of the single friend is also his love of the world, as in *The Merchant of Venice*[10] Solanio says of Antonio.[11] And how rashly Cassius seizes the words of Brutus in which this one seeks to excuse his bitter behavior; how fast he himself admits that he inherited a rash humor from his mother!

Here follows now one of those masterstrokes of Shakespeare which he learned from nature. A poet enters who wants to reconcile the generals, an apparently useless, superfluous, accidental figure. For long I could not explain to myself his appearance, and even now I do not know whether I have interpreted it correctly.

As, of course, friends, after a serious quarrel, seek to outdo themselves in reciprocal kindnesses: so both here change, as it were, their nature and speak from the sense of the other. The art-loving Brutus shows the poet his way; Cassius, the rough, serious warrior excuses him and pleads for him. The impression is touching and expresses the highest reconciliation, the complete settlement of the unhappy argument.

The following scenes, where both souls, as it were, dive into one another, where Cassius is full of deep sympathy for Brutus, full of pride at his even-tempered friend, where both cannot conceive

---

8   IV. iii, 97–99. Where I have translated "learns them by heart," the German has "lernt sie aus dem Kopf" – "learns them from the head" or "learns them from the top."

9   IV. iii, 101–2.

10   Translator's italics.

11   *The Merchant of Venice*, II. viii, 50.

their previous mistakes, then that leave-taking in the night, where they only grudgingly part and say again and again farewell, then Brutus' conversation with the sleep-drunk Lucius, in which he thinks so often of his "brother" Cassius, up until the appearance of Caesar as a ghost, the last, horrible warning about past and future – these scenes come before me, like the last part of a symphony, in which the same notes, which in the Allegro stormed and flashed, again resound, but almost as a painful sigh in remembrance of the endured woes, almost as transfigured and calmed tones of a breast become silent.

The fixed defiance of Cassius in the face of gods and human beings sinks even before his end, his Epicurean system staggers within him, he knows, that his death is near and even believes in the omen that proclaims this to him. He even does not resist Brutus, who wants to leave a favorable position and put everything into play in one decisive battle. "Let the gods be kind to us today," he says, in that he takes leave of his friend forever, "so that we associate, in peace approaching old age."[12] But he doubts a happy ending, and this doubt justifies the result.

The error, "melancholy's child, mistrusting a good ending,"[13] occasions his sad end, the error, that is always fatefully engaged in his life, that even finally was able so easily to negate his friendship. "My life has been brought full circle,"[14] he cries out, he thinks on his birthday, "satisfied with the earthy confines, to release life."[15]

His last words are an atonement for his whole life; they touch the last dark point of his inner self, which he never wanted to confess to himself, at which he never hinted in conversation with others, the reproach that weighs upon his heart since Caesar's assassination. "Caesar, thou art reveng'd, and with the same sword that killed thee."[16] It is possible that this dark place first became noticeable at

12   V. i, 93–94.
13   V. iii, 74–75.
14   V. iii, 25.
15   I. iii, 99–100.
16   V. iii, 45–47.

the last moment, it is possible that his unhappiness since that fateful deed opened his eyes to it – surely these words, these little words, which throw a sudden glancing light on the most concealed furrows of his heart, have something deeply moving and stirring and wipe out of our soul that last ill humor, the last loathing of his character. –

Goethe narrates in his *Italian Journey*,[17] what peculiar enchantment the song of the gondoliers in Venice practiced on him: "Like a voice out of the distance," he says, "it sounds strange in the highest degree, like a lament without sadness; it is therein something unbelievable, touching to the point of tears." We feel similarly when we, so to speak, hear sounding out through the distance a deep human passion through the fetters into which the will force of a human being or the pressure of circumstances slapped them; it is the human, that forces its way through the night of melancholy times like a distant song to our heart.

A friendship of two men, in the disorders of upheavals of the state, which, dragged into the maelstrom of party struggles, hazards and sacrifices its most beloved, the one the most heartfelt love of a man whom the other hates, the other his strong will and his political wisdom, in order to satisfy the heart of the friend: a friendship of this kind, which burdens both with error and guilt, draws both into destruction, has also something unendingly touching. Such a friendship is that of Brutus and Cassius, it is the soul of the whole piece, that represents, as we otherwise do not find with Shakespeare, the struggle of common human and moral motives with political ones. Let us observe overall what depths Shakespeare puts into the friendships portrayed by him: Bassanio, who "would like to sacrifice his life, his wife, and all the world in order to free Antonio,"[18] and Cassius who becomes untrue to his

---

17   My italics; Goethe, *Italienishce Reise*, entry dated 6 October. Where Goethe's text has "etwas unglaublich" (something unbelievably), Nietzsche's quotation has "etwas Unglaubliches" (something unbelievable), changing an adverb into a noun.

18   *The Merchant of Venice*, IV. i, 282.

fixed character and to his conviction when Brutus wants other than he, – they let us cast a glimpse at Shakespeare's mind, even as it stands firm historically, which lifelong holds itself open toward friendship.

SUGGESTED SECONDARY READING

Cooper, David E. *Authenticity and Learning: Nietzsche's Educational Philosophy*. Boston: Routledge and Kegan Paul, 1983.

Derrida, Jacques. *The Ear of the Other*. New York: Schocken Books, 1985.

Golomb, Jacob. "Nietzsche's Early Educational Thought." *Journal of Philosophy of Education*, 19(1), 99–109, 1985.

Gossman, Lionel. *Basel in the Age of Burckhardt*. Chicago: University of Chicago Press, 2000.

Havenstein, Martin. *Nietzsche als Erzieher*. Berlin: E. S. Mittler und Sohn, 1922.

Heilke, Thomas. *Nietzsche's Tragic Regime*. Dekalb: Northern Illinois University Press, 1998.

Janz, Curt Paul. *Friedrich Nietzsche: Biographie*. 3 vols. Munich: Deutscher Taschenbuch Verlag, 1981.

Löw, Reinhard. *Nietzsche: Sophist und Erzieher*. Weinheim: Acta humaniora, 1984.

Murphy, Timothy. *Nietzsche as Educator*. Lanham, Md.: University Press of America, 1984.

Peters, Michael, James Marshall and Paul Smeyers, editors. *Nietzsche's Legacy for Education: Past and Present Values*. Westport, Conn.: Bergin and Garvey, 2001.

Pletsch, Carl. *Young Nietzsche: Becoming a genius*. New York: The Free Press, 1991.

Porter, James I. *Nietzsche and the Philology of the Future.* Stanford: Stanford University Press, 2000.

Rosenow, E. "Nietzsche's Concept of Education." In *Nietzsche as Affirmative Thinker,* ed. Yirmiyahu Yovel. Dordrecht: Martinus Nijhoff, 1986.

Schneider, J. "Nietzsche's basler Vorträge 'Über die Zukunft unserer Bildungsanstalten' in licht seiner Lektüre pädagogischer Schriften." *Nietzsche Studien,* 21, 308–25, 1992.

Shapiro, Gary. "Nietzsche and the Future of the University." *Journal of Nietzsche Studies,* 1, 15–28, 1991.

Taylor, Quentin P. *The Republic of Genius: A Reconstruction of Nietzsche's Early Thought.* Rochester: University of Rochester Press, 1997.

INDEX